falling&
laughing

falling&laughing

The Restoration of Edwyn Collins

GRACE MAXWELL

EBURY
PRESS

3 5 7 9 10 8 6 4 2

Published in 2009 by Ebury Press, an imprint of Ebury Publishing
A Random House Group company

The Random House Group Limited Reg. No. 954009

Addresses for companies within the Random House Group can be found at
www.randomhouse.co.uk

A CIP catalogue record for this book is available from the British Library

The Random House Group Limited supports The Forest Stewardship
Council (FSC), the leading international forest certification organisation.
All our titles that are printed on Greenpeace approved FSC certified paper
carry the FSC logo. Our paper procurement policy can be found at
www.rbooks.co.uk/environment

Mixed Sources
Product group from well-managed
forests and other controlled sources
www.fsc.org Cert no. TT-COC-2139
© 1996 Forest Stewardship Council

Designed and set by seagulls.net

Printed and bound in Great Britain by Clays Ltd, St Ives PLC

ISBN 9780091929992

To buy books by your favourite authors and register for offers visit
www.rbooks.co.uk

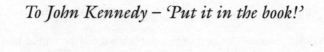

To John Kennedy – 'Put it in the book!'

PROLOGUE · AUGUST 2005

ON OUR USUAL drive from Northwick Park Hospital to Harrow town centre for supper, Edwyn stuns me by bursting into song.

> 'I'm searching for the truth
> I'm searching for the truth
> Some sweet day we'll get there in the end
> Some sweet day we'll get there in the end.'

A song which has sprung from nowhere, he sings it over and over as I transfer him to his wheelchair and push him to our regular haunt. Our choices are limited by the chair, and the unlovely pedestrianised shopping centre location, but Nandos has tasty free-range chicken and good access. Edwyn is in full celebratory voice all the way there, and all the way back. After six indescribably weird months, he's due to leave hospital for good in two days, so I christen it his demob song. Back on the ward, he sings it to Mark, his last remaining room-mate. Soon the two of them are belting it out together.

Mark was here before Edwyn and will be there when we've gone. He remembers our first meeting. Edwyn was stuck on a phrase at that time (something that has been a feature of his speech and language affliction), but I can't remember what it was. Mark does: 'The possibilities are endless. The possibilities are endless ...'

•

I AM COMPOSED of my thoughts. Imagine it. Suddenly there are no more thoughts. Your brain doesn't work properly. The damage is such that you barely know who you are, the nature of your existence. The loss of your intellect, your wit, doesn't begin to describe it.

The way it was for Edwyn, for Edwyn and me, was deeper and stranger. Before we could even think about his cleverness, his fabulous sarcasm, his highly developed sense of the absurd (where they had gone? Were they coming back?), we had to wrestle with questions of simple identity.

It's impossible to imagine what it felt like to be inside Edwyn's brain as he struggled to return to awareness, to self-knowledge. He describes it thus: 'I was peaceful and tranquil at first. No thoughts at all. Edwyn Collins, that's me, I knew that. But everything else, it's gone.'

Brain damage was an especial dread. For two years I would not even utter the words. I used any euphemism I could think of to avoid describing what had happened to

Edwyn in these unthinkable terms. Edwyn was much more courageous. His honesty had not deserted him, nor his bluntness. He confronted his new self unflinchingly. 'Brain damage, I think. I'm a moron.'

EARLY DAYS

EDWYN COLLINS IS Scottish and so am I, but we are also Londoners. I came to the big smoke from Scotland in 1980, escaping a Glasgow that seemed cliquish and defensive. There were a lot of west of Scotland 'flat-earthers' around then: they thought you fell off the world at the end of the M8. When I return to Glasgow these days I can barely recognise it. There is a very different, self-confident atmosphere and I remember all the things about the city that I loved.

I met Edwyn for the first time in my living room in Willesden, in north-west London, on a Sunday evening in August, three months after my arrival in London. A friend from Glasgow called and asked if I could put two people up for a few days (on the floor). Edwyn was the singer in a band called Orange Juice who, together with my other guest, Alan Horne, had set up an indie label called Postcard Records of Scotland, primarily as a route to release Orange Juice records. Edwyn was tall, gangly and the most voluble of the two. Alan was a little shorter, a little rounder and had the spikier personality. They looked great, particularly Edwyn, dressed in an old-fashioned and out-of-step-with-the-times tweedy style crafted from market stalls and charity shops. Dapper and original. Neither of them drank or smoked. They had beautiful manners and a brilliant way with an anecdote. Stories and gossip, exaggerations and embellishments, a deadly eye for the absurd in every human sketch. The purpose of their mission to London was to drum up attention for the band and their fledgling label.

The sales approach for the first Orange Juice single, a song that Edwyn wrote when he was seventeen called 'Falling and Laughing', was to pack the boxes in the back of Alan's dad's Austin Maxi and travel the length and breadth of the UK, calling in at all the independent record stores they found listed in the back pages of music papers. (After one trip to London in the Maxi, the windscreen blew in just a few miles up the M1 on the way home. Rather than stop and bear the expense of getting it fixed, or maybe because they just didn't have the money, they drove all the way back to Glasgow with no windscreen. It was raining, and even hailing, at one point. *For four hundred miles.* Complete madness. Apparently, Edwyn was crouched on the floor in the back, sheltering from the weather, until Alan made him come up the front to suffer alongside him.)

Going for the direct, straight-to-the-counter sales approach for 'Falling and Laughing' would result in on the spot transactions of maybe two copies, ten copies or, in one spectacular success, a hundred. I think they had pressed 1,000 and were soon sold out. Today, it's a rarity

early days

of great price. Edwyn and I don't possess a single copy, like most of his records, which is common among musicians. You give them all away. It's traditional, and if you end up with none left for yourself, that's just the way it is. It doesn't matter a bit.

•

IN MY LIVING room on that Sunday in August, Edwyn and Alan made an arresting double act. It's very difficult to accurately describe at this distance of time the effect of their company. They were very young, very clever and very funny. They made a compelling, mesmerising impression. A journalist and DJ from Glasgow, Billy Sloan, who knew them at the time and who we are still in contact with, remembers the Postcard fraternity as being a right bunch of smartasses, very bright, but also intimidating. You took your life in your hands, somewhat, in attempting to interview them. While sarkiness was their stock in trade (Steven Daly, the erstwhile drummer and manager, reckons that they used the bulk of their energies in thinking up the next great put-down rather than concentrating on pushing the band and the label forward), they were terribly quick on the draw, deft and articulate, and could be disarmingly charming.

Much what I write here concerns human fragility and even mortality, but, at this time, these two rather extraordinary boys represented the polar opposite, overflowing as they did with vitality, thrilling with the invincibility of youth and the knowledge that they were in the moment. They certainly knew their time was coming and were brimful of exuberance and self-confidence.

Edwyn has described to me how he would lie awake dreaming up schemes and plans to advance the cause of his band and the label. Alan would be doing the same. Everybody stuck their oars in, a result of which, in retrospect, Edwyn thinks the label may have suffered from a surfeit of ideas, which ultimately contributed to its downfall In fact it existed for no more than two years, folding in late 1981. For the enduring fans of the music produced by this precocious label, the draw was not just in the music but in the ideas, the debate even, behind them. The music business and the majority of the record buying public can't be doing with too cerebral an approach to pop music. But for the Postcard boys pop music was a deadly serious business, and they aired their often conflicting ideas with one another and the public, like any healthy art movement would.

Over the years as Edwyn's manager, I have been asked quite often for advice from bands or individuals about the best way to grab the attention of the music business and secure a record deal. My heart sinks, because I have no blueprint for approaching record companies, cap in hand. Having watched Edwyn and co. in action, it's a case of if you have to ask how it's done, it's probably not for you. Edwyn and his Postcard compadres made up their own version of the music business and were scathing about the proper one. Because they knew the conventional business would never invite them to their party, they snubbed it and convened their own, and it became the one that everybody wanted to come to.

•

THAT MONDAY MORNING in August 1980, Edwyn and Alan were up with the lark. As I was getting ready to set off for work on my moped (I was a house manager in a theatre), they were on their way, on foot, to walk the four miles to London's West End in order to lay siege to music papers and magazines. With no appointments in advance, they achieved all they set out to. I remember how dismissive they were of the scene they saw before them at each magazine office. Seas of hippies behind their desks. They also planned to waylay the influential radio DJ John Peel. Far from attempting to ingratiate themselves, Alan was keen to explain to him the error of his ways. The precise quote was, I believe, 'Wise up, old man ...'

It was all tremendous, mischievous fun; the hallmark of Orange Juice and Postcard Records. But the music was powerfully seductive too and made the label one of the most influential around for a long time. The records left their mark and still speak to young people today. A musical critique would be impossible here: suffice to say, the early work is rather wonderful.

Soon the Willesden pad was a stopping-over base for the rest of the band and others from the label when they came to London to play gigs or promote records. Edwyn and Alan had persuaded Aztec Camera to record for the label and Roddy Frame, the preposterously talented front-man, came to stay. He was seventeen years old, a proper prodigy as a musician and songwriter. I remember his excitement at acquiring his first posh vintage guitar on that trip and again, in true Postcard visitor style, his beautiful manners. This may seem unusual behaviour for fledgling rock stars, but Postcard Records was all about going against the grain. Rock posturing was studiously avoided. TVs were never thrown from windows, drug taking was for old men and as for cavorting with groupies, perish the thought. Theirs was not a moral standpoint, simply that it had been done to death. The Postcard men rejected all behaviour they considered clichéd, hackneyed, boring.

●

I FIRST SAW Orange Juice play live at the famous Marquee Club in Wardour Street, in the autumn of 1980, supporting a band called The Associates. Edwyn told me, years later, that he was mildly surprised that night to see that in the period since we had last met, I'd transformed myself from a hippy to a skinhead. I'd foolishly allowed myself to be lured into a hairdressing training session on South Molton Street on the promise of a free haircut. The guy I was assigned to had suggested an 'asymmetrical theme'. I had no clue what he was on about but, because I was clearly mad back then, I agreed. I ended up with a creation that was up and down like Gourock, as we say in Glasgow. A ludicrous 80s confection; a cross between the Human League and A Flock of Seagulls, with shaved bits, long bits and pointy bits. I lived with the hideousness for a week and then took the only course open to me, which was to have the whole lot shaved off. I was now a bleached-blonde skinhead, a bit like Toyah in her young, fat face incarnation, as the punky star of Derek Jarman's film, *Jubilee* (unsurprisingly, this pre-dated the genesis of Edwyn's fancying me).

To see Edwyn's band play back then was a rare and

wonderful thing. I'm probably not the best person to attempt to describe what they were like; there are lots of music writers who have made a much better job of it than I could. But the main thing for me was the absence of clichés. They couldn't play expertly, but they did play beautifully. The tunes were gorgeous. The words were clever and funny and self-effacing. They used to say they were 'anti-rock'. In the early days, Glasgow audiences used to chant 'Poofs! Poofs! Poofs!' at them. They liked that just fine. There was a campness in their delivery, deliberately affected to annoy the manly men of rock. James Kirk, who also sang, played guitar and wrote songs alongside Edwyn, was a particular wonder, the like of which I've never seen before or since. To go back in time and tape some of his occasional on-stage anecdotes would be a delight for me in my old age.

IN NOVEMBER 2008, the band members, Edwyn, James, Steven Daly and David McClymont were reunited for the first time in twenty-five years, to pick up an award, sponsored by the music therapy charity, Nordoff Robbins, in Glasgow recognising the impact they made on music at the time, and its reverberations down the years. James still makes music, David has lived and worked as a journalist in Melbourne for twenty years and Steven is a contributing editor to *Vanity Fair* in New York. All grown up, but they seemed to fall back into the same patterns with one another almost immediately. Accepting the award, James described a gig at Maryhill Town Hall in Glasgow where Edwyn played with his arm in a sling. He had been beaten up in

Kelvingrove Park (Alan had been with him but had hero-ically run away!). At the gig, the audience kept shouting out for Showaddywaddy numbers and banging their pool cues on the stage in a menacing way. Orange Juice's sartorial flair and their out of kilter musical style was confusing the punters and they weren't best pleased. This was a full force ned (a Glasgow word for a guy who's up for a fight) reac-tion to the weird, un-Glasgowness of the band. The lads obliged with a blast of 'Standing in the corner in my new blue jeans' (from 'Hey Rock 'n' Roll'). James said Edwyn was the definition of grace under pressure that night, which rather neatly describes the original line-up of Orange Juice.

They excelled at stage patter, James and Edwyn. James' stories would be accompanied by Edwyn's convulsive laugh, a bizarre noise that those who have heard it in the flesh will agree defies description. As James told the story that November night, Edwyn stood beside him doing the laugh, and for me, the years fell away.

·

TIME MOVES FAST and this version of Orange Juice burned very brightly for a short time before falling apart in a confu-sion of wounded egos and intemperate decision-making. Looking back on how short the actual time period was – maybe a year and a half – it scarcely seems enough time to have had such an impact. I wish I'd been their manager then. I would have tried very hard to prevent the original members from falling apart. In my arrogance, perhaps, I believe I could have been the sensible and impartial parental figure. I still think they are all brilliant people, dazzling originals.

EDWYN & GRACE

BY THE TIME Edwyn and I became good friends again in 1983, he was something of a pop star, although his band had been reduced to a nucleus of him and a drummer, Zeke Manyika. The signs weren't good. I was still working in a theatre as a house manager, something I'd done for years, both in Glasgow and London. I'd bumped into Edwyn from time to time over the intervening period, and followed the band's fortunes, but we really only became very friendly when he moved into my old house with the two photographers who had always lived there, and I was in my newly renovated, one-bedroom flat down the road in Kensal Green. For me, this was a thrilling time. After about ten house moves and millions of flatmates, I was finally on my own. I had been a member of a housing co-operative since I first came to London and it had finally provided me with my own place. Edwyn was a regular visitor and I became his confidante. I'd listen to his love life complications, feigning concern, while secretly finding his tribulations ridiculously adolescent. But on other subjects, he was a fascinating, instructive and hilarious companion. He had an interesting angle on everything and I learned so much from him.

In early 1984, Edwyn and Orange Juice were without a manager and he asked me if I wanted the job. Of course, I wasn't remotely qualified for the position, but the thought of self-employment was very appealing and I accepted. I think he may have been regretting his decision even as he was offering, but I gave him no opportunity to change his mind; after years of easy friendship Edwyn had developed a fancy for me and this was actually the true motivation for the job offer. He denied it for years, but I finally got him to admit his weakness. I hadn't set my cap at him, pop star or no. I was dimly aware that this might have been at the back of his mind, but I was happy to let events unfold as they may. I didn't see Edwyn and myself in that light. If it became a problem I assumed I'd get the sack. But I was deluded enough to think I'd be an excellent manager.

I sped through a crash course in the structure of the business life of Orange Juice, helped mainly by the terrific figure of Paul Rodwell, Edwyn's lawyer and a true gentleman. He was, sadly, a rose among thorns. It turned out, to my utter astonishment, that the music business was populated by misogynists and sexists. Men that were uncomfortable around women, basically. Coming from my illuminated, egalitarian theatre world, I think I had a skewed idea of the progress the world was making. I have never seen secretaries spoken to in the way they were in record companies. I was quite shocked.

Edwyn introduced me to the personnel at Polydor Records, where he had been representing himself for a short time. He would waltz in wearing a houndstooth overcoat, carrying a brolly and an old-fashioned, battered briefcase.

'Hello Edwyn! How are you today?' the girls in the outer office would ask.

'I'm very well, thank you, my dear, and may I ask what you've been doing for my band Orange Juice today?' Mass giggling all round.

One of the first meetings I attended as Orange Juice's manager was with a fairly arrogant character who was in charge of international relations. He began to lecture Edwyn about his lack of touring activity abroad. Edwyn wasn't mad keen on touring in those days, and Zeke was an illegal immigrant, originally from Zimbabwe, who had overstayed his student visa by about six years and who no longer had a passport of any type.

'The bottom line is, Edwyn, that unless you have a career abroad, you will end up with no career.'

'Don't fucking "bottom line" me, pal,' Edwyn had snarled back. I listened wide eyed as he continued, starting to get more of an idea of what I had got myself into.

It's amazing to recall how unperturbed I was as the depths of the problems with his record company unfolded. At this time, Edwyn was my job, not my family, and everything was funny. The next few months were like living in a daft sitcom – it was just what you would think being the manager of a pop star would be like. I was woefully inexperienced, but I was learning as I trailed around in the wake of my eccentric teacher. I even began tour managing at the back end of the year. The job of the tour manager is all-encompassing. Advance planning, musicians, crew, venue logistics, PA, lights, transport, hotels, catering, detailed itinerary, budgeting, accounting. Everyone on tour, especially musicians, can be needy and the buck stops with the tour manager. Later, for reasons of economy, I expanded my role to bus driver. I used to tell Edwyn that if we got really desperate, I'd become a long distance lorry driver. I enjoyed it.

I doubt Edwyn would have recommended a career as a driver for me, though. In the first year I worked for him we spent a lot of time together criss-crossing London in the 'company car', a second-hand VW Golf. These journeys were hilarious. Edwyn would go into character (my favourite was a Glaswegian hairdresser called 'Angelo Morocco') and keep up a running commentary. Probably because I was in fits, we had several bumps and scrapes. My favourite trick was reversing into parked cars.

'You've just hit that car, you know.'

'That doesn't count. It's just a touch. Everybody does that.'

Edwyn took to screaming 'Touch!!!' every time I did it after that.

On day I was delivering a lengthy lecture about car drivers and their disregard of motorcyclists. As I was in mid-flow we pulled up at traffic lights alongside a motorbike. The rider began knocking on Edwyn's passenger window in an agitated fashion, pointing frantically towards the ground. It turned out I'd trapped his leg against the car. Perfect comedy timing.

Back at the record company, Polydor, relations were deteriorating. At one point, in high dudgeon over a perceived lack of interest in his forthcoming album, Edwyn asked me to convene a meeting with the head of the company. This gentleman was a tremendous character, terrifically old school, very courtly, with a penthouse apartment on the top floor of Polydor's HQ. (He wasn't long for the job as it turned out as he was soon transferred to a classical division, which I'm sure would have been a happy move.) But Edwyn had a sympathetic relationship with him and I had no trouble setting up the meeting.

I arrived first, and was greeted with great courtesy as AJ (his first name) enquired as to the reason for the meeting. I was able to fill him in a little before Edwyn blew in, fashionably late (his record back then was a whole four hours), tall and resplendent in a 1950s, camel-coloured, double-breasted Prince of Wales check suit with wide lapels and a turquoise sweater, topped off by his mad quiffed hairdo. I blinked at the sight of this vision of loveliness, but AJ rose graciously to meet him and we got right down to business.

'Now, Edwyn, Grace has been telling me about how aggrieved you've been feeling lately.'

'AJ, I can sum up my feelings in one word.' Edwyn raised his hand and brought it down on the table as he thundered dramatically, 'Betrayed!'

Somehow, I maintained my composure. I will never know how.

By the end of November 1984 Edwyn had completed the last of four Orange Juice albums, which he called *The Third Album*. (More eccentric, or absurdist, behaviour. Or as Polydor would have put it, annoying.) He decided he wanted to advertise it on TV. This was never going to happen. Record companies don't normally fork out for expensive television advertising even for groups they

1985

like and Polydor was no different. But we found a way ourselves. We funded a limited run on Channel 4 at Christmas time and I was cut some very nifty deals. We made the ad ourselves with the help of a Channel 4 Films producer called Sarah Radcliffe, who did it for nothing because she liked Edwyn and is a genuinely brilliant person. We had met her when she produced the last-ever Orange Juice video for a song called 'What Presence?!' that was directed by the famous British avant garde film director Derek Jarman. Working with Derek on the video was the greatest pleasure, the most ridiculous fun it is possible to have at work. Later, when I needed some advice about making the advert, I turned to Sarah, and she simply took over. How wonderful. It was directed by Nic and Luc Roeg, sons of the film director, Nicolas Roeg, and consisted of Edwyn holding a large fish, and introducing his new album. Cut to Zeke who intones, seriously: 'Which includes the flop singles, 'What Presence?!' and 'Lean Period'.'

All this as the word FLOP! flashed up on the screen continuously.

We never imagined it would help sales much. Edwyn was content to throw his own money at an elaborate wind-up of the record company. We were young and foolish and ever so slightly petty, and it had to be done.

So, that was that with Polydor, as you can imagine.

•

THE ENSUING TEN or so years were up and down for Edwyn on the career front. Strangely though, in retrospect, I can barely remember the periods of penury; when I was reluctant to answer the phone or open letters to find what fresh hell lurked inside. All the bad stuff was punctuated by adventure and enormous creativity. That's what I remember. Hurtling from one daft sketch to another. We invariably managed to find a way to survive each mini crisis, which in turn steels you for the next.

Edwyn moved into my little flat one item at a time. One day I turned around and all his worldly goods were there in their entirety, although I had no recollection of how they had arrived. I had formerly been a proto-minimalist: the fewer possessions, the easier to move, the less to clean up. My new flat had been spacious and empty, but, alas, those days were gone for good. As I surveyed piles of Edwyn's eclectic stuff, the battle lines for the next twenty years were drawn between the hoarder and the chucker.

I operated from the illustrious surroundings of our living room, conducting all business cross-legged on the floor. There was no room for a desk. If I was out, in order to maintain a semblance of professionalism, or more likely just for naughtiness' sake, Edwyn would pretend to be my cockney PA, Dave.

'Grace isn't available, this is Dave, her assistant. Well, I'm not really *orfarised* to make those decisions. But I'll pass it on to the organ grinder when she gets back.'

Later, when callers would revisit their conversations with Dave, I would struggle to hold it together. Eventually I started to behave as if my imaginary PA really existed.

•

NOW A SOLO artist, we struggled to find a record company willing to support him. Edwyn's music still came as easily and naturally as it ever did, but he had made a fair few enemies in his time and we were up against it. We toured quite a bit, in the UK and around Europe, with me as tour manager and sometime bus driver. I only gave up after our son, William, was born, completing my last tour behind the wheel when I was six months pregnant. But eventually, in 1989, we were able to get Edwyn's career somewhat back on track when he was invited to record an album for a German label, Werk, at their superbly appointed studios in Cologne. Edwyn relocated to the city for three months, together with various members of his band and old friends, including our friend Roddy Frame, and the Orange Juice producer and famous reggae maestro, Dennis Bovell. These were wonderfully happy days, with Edwyn at his best, collaborating intensely with much-loved fellow musicians, with no animosity or rivalry. The result was just as he had hoped. I drove a transit van from London to Cologne at the end of the process, in order to transport the instruments back. I remember arriving in the dead of night, with Edwyn and Tomgor the producer waiting up, dying to play me the fruits of the labours.

With this quite successful album called *Hope and Despair*, things started to take a turn for the better.

•

BY 1992, we were still living in my old flat in Kensal Green, still broke, but pretty happy. William had been born in 1990 and I always feel he brought us a lot of luck. Edwyn had begun to produce records for other bands and was hell-bent on acquiring a studio of his own. This was the only way he would be free to make records, without having to go cap in hand to a record company for permission to do so. We reckoned that the law of diminishing returns had come into effect as far as the record business advancing Edwyn money was concerned. With each approach to the powers that be, there seemed to be increasing reluctance to involve themselves with Edwyn's recording career. In short, we couldn't get arrested, and we were quite weary of the dance. I was thirty-four years old, Edwyn thirty-two, and it didn't seem very dignified at our time of life to go begging to idiots for the right to record. We were great at doing things on a shoestring, had had lots of practise in recent years, and were determined to find a way to plough our own furrow, unencumbered by the expectations of what Edwyn used to sarkily refer to as 'The Industry of Human Happiness'.

Bit by bit, Edwyn had been acquiring pieces of vintage recording equipment, centred around a Neve console, or mixing desk, from 1969 (with the famous 1064 and 1073 modules – he's always bragging about them), picked up for a song from the defunct Goldcrest Film Studios in London's Soho. As tedious as it may sound to outsiders, acquiring and learning about this old gear had virtually become the Meaning of Life to Edwyn. Next to his baby son, that is.

A vintage equipment dealer and producer named Mark Thompson, whom Edwyn met a year or so later, had helped him find the adored mixing desk. Together they set up home in a converted coach house at Alexandra Palace, pooling equipment and splitting the rent. The birthing process was long and fraught and, for us, set against a financial background that was, frankly, farcical. Looking back, I have no clue how we survived this period of keeping the studio going, and living on thin air. I do recall doing the sums at one stage and Edwyn asking me how much longer we could survive. 'Until two months ago. Press on.'

•

A RECORDING STUDIO is a complicated technical environment which requires very specific specialist skills to put together. At its hub is a recording console, or desk, which receives the music from the microphones, treats it, colours it, manipulates it, with the help of umpteen other bits of gear we call 'outboard', and transfers it to tape. Or that's how it used to work. Nowadays it will go to a computer hard drive. (Edwyn still swears by tape). The specialist guys who cable this lot together are, in my experience, a strange bunch who inhabit a parallel universe and are impossible to tie down to budgets or timescales. But where there is a will there is a way. And when it all comes together, you need a gifted engineer to operate it.

And this was when the beautiful thing that is Sebastian Lewsley came into Edwyn's life. They had met a year or so back, when Edwyn spent time at a studio in Chiswick called Sonnet. Seb was nineteen and the studio owner had been ruthlessly exploiting Seb's youth, enthusiasm and talent, although Seb did learn a lot in the process. It was a very funny place, frequented by old lags of the music industry, such as Shakin' Stevens, the bloke from Sailor, and the brilliant Anthony Newley, providing Seb with a rich seam of comedy that he mines to this day. Edwyn and Seb are wont to slip into character, as Jackson Gold and Denny Lorimar, two old-school music producers, bitter old dinosaurs, boring for Britain. This pair, based as they are on real-life weirdos that have been part of Edwyn and Seb's past, have made an indelible impression on every client who has passed through our studio in the last fourteen years or so. Nobody escapes; all are sucked into the sad world of Jackson and Denny. People have come to speak of them as if they really exist.

In 1999, Channel 4 commissioned a sit-com based on the pair's imagined exploits. Six episodes and a one-hour special were made. The storylines, risible as they were, were sketched out in advance, but the dialogue was entirely improvised. A huge cast of characters, composed entirely of friends and colleagues, (for example, Jamal, our accountant, played Jamal, the accountant) rose magnificently to the challenge. It aired late at night, and was re-run, garnering Jackson and Denny a tiny but fanatical following. One day soon, it will resurface.

Edwyn asked Seb to leave Sonnet behind to come and join him, and they learned the new studio together. Ever since then Edwyn has spent much more of his waking, working life with Seb than he has with me. They have learned to communicate telepathically which, in the circumstances, has proven to be handy.

The arrangement at the first studio was a six-week-turnaround type of thing. In early 1994, the studio was finally ready and Edwyn spent the first six weeks producing an album for a band called the Rockingbirds, which would finance the next few months and allow him to work on his own album when it was his turn to use the studio.

Finally, in May, recording got under way. The whole thing took six weeks from start to finish, with no remixes. One particular track was recorded in two days. Very easy, according to Edwyn, and not bad for the song that made us our fortune, changed our lives and continues to support us to this day. The song was called 'A Girl Like You', and it's much more famous than Edwyn. In America, loads of people think it was a David Bowie record, or an Iggy Pop record. I'm not sure why but it's true.

The track was recorded, written and produced by Edwyn. Two of his heroes and dear friends, Paul Cook of the Sex Pistols and Vic Godard of the Subway Sect, played on it, as did Clare Kenny and Sean Read. All brilliant musicians, and also the very first pick you would make for fantastic people to share a session with.

Edwyn has been incredibly fortunate to have the song's protection at his back through the most challenging years I hope we'll ever have to face. How lucky it is to have resources to ensure that whatever he needs, he gets. And I have not had to give up my job to look after him. He is my job. We are acutely aware that most people who find themselves in similar circumstances don't have our options. They have to take what's on offer and that, I'm afraid, is pretty much a lottery (but even at its best, it's often rubbish).

Did Edwyn have a glimmer that lurking on this album was a track that would turn his life around? Not at all. We did think it sounded like a potential single, but a hit? We had thought lots of his previous singles were potential hits but we had proved to be all too wrong. In our minds, unless you had a fairly souped-up industry engine on your side, your chances were less than slim.

As it turned out, we were almost right.

At the end of the recording sessions for the album, called *Gorgeous George*, Mark announced that he wanted the studio to himself and had negotiated a new lease with the landlady, so we were immediately out on our ear. No bad thing as it transpired, because life was about to become so frenetic that the additional burden of running the studio wouldn't have helped. So, Edwyn completed the recording of his album and the very next day we moved the equipment out. This is always a ghastly process, even though I am an accomplished removals expert. By necessity, certainly not by choice. I loathe it. Once more we turned to our trusty removers, my neighbour, Big Phil, and his sidekick, Mad Tony. They called the business (assets: one transit van) Caledonian Removals, and they had the best business card in the world. Under the company name was their motto:

'We Don't Fuck About.'

Which they did, actually, quite a lot. Top quality.

The gear went into storage and we set about finding a release for the record.

We licensed the record for the UK and a couple of other territories to a tiny independent label called Setanta, run from a squat in Camberwell, south London, by a Dubliner called Keith Cullen. This would be a real collaborative effort, as the label was even less experienced than we, and we were all ill-equipped to deal with the juggernaut of 'A Girl Like You'.

The record was released as a single in November 1994 and entered the chart at no 43, I think. Or 45. Anyway, not a hit. Business as usual, we thought. So near and yet so far. Oh well. But then an odd thing happened. It wouldn't go away. As the year drew to a close, the track was getting increasingly more airplay and we received news of radio stations picking up on it in Europe and Australia – countries where it had not yet been released – so, airplay in countries where we had no record company yet. Something was up, and it had nothing to do with my business acumen.

In late February 1995 we travelled to Australia for a twelve day promotional blitz to support the increasing success of 'A Girl Like You'. I don't recommend this journey. Australia is too far away to go for anything less than a month. I have never known jet lag like it, akin to a bad flu. Edwyn worked extremely hard, performing five shows with a band of musicians assembled for him by the record company (great guys who were perfectly rehearsed when we got there) and doing about a hundred interviews. William, aged four, coped far better than we did. When sleep overcame him, he just dropped wherever he was. I would bring pillows from the hotel and make a nest for him in the dressing rooms, where he would snooze happily, undisturbed by the cacophony going on around him.

On the way home we parted company with Edwyn at Hong Kong airport. He was to fly on to Los Angeles while we returned to London. We would join him in Austin, Texas, five days later. This was Edwyn's first ever trip to the US. In LA, he was scheduled to perform acoustically three days later at the famous Viper Room, once co-owned by Johnny Depp. On his arrival, he decided to go down there to check it out. Combining a few drinks with his jet lag and travel weariness, he sat at the bar. When a couple of girls started chatting to him, he responded, charming them with his delightful Scottish accent. Their boyfriends, a couple of muscly jock types, weren't so charmed and let him know it. I don't know what he said back but I believe it involved some old-fashioned Glasgow-style cursing, and moments later he was on the floor, felled by a blow to the face. He had only been in America for three hours and he'd managed to get into a fight. In the Viper Room. When he called me later that night, feeling very sorry for himself, his two black eyes were already developing nicely.

The next day he met up with an old friend of mine, Neil Fraser, who had married an LA girl and become a California lawyer. Neil planned to take Edwyn guitar shopping at a market in Pasadena. They stopped off at his home first and as he was reversing the car down the driveway they both felt the back wheel crunch over something. Neil had run over Bingo, the family dog. A quick dash to the vet later and poor Bingo had to be put to sleep. Edwyn watched awkwardly as Neil broke the news to his two small daughters who, although initially distraught, rallied at the thought of a replacement for Bingo.

'We want a Chihuahua! We want a Chihuahua!'

When I received the call updating me on Day Two, I started to panic about Day Three. I begged him to stay in his room until the show. Will and I met him two days later at the airport in Austin and got our first look at his impressive shiners. They were still in evidence when we reached New York a few days later. He performed his acoustic set in three locations, allowing some of his small but devoted band of American supporters to see him play for the first time. In New York Edwyn's favourite aunt, Kate Mackintosh (who had lived there for twenty-odd years), was our guest of honour. She had never seen him perform before and was mesmerized both by Edwyn's stage persona and the audience reaction ('Wee Eddie, is that really him?'). These memorable shows were enhanced by his hysterically funny and rambling rendition of his LA adventures. He took to the stage wearing dark glasses which required explanation. Revealing the damage created a dramatic flourish.

By summertime 1995, we had a huge record on our hands. It was never a case of thinking of ways to make it happen, more of running to try and catch up with the damn thing. A phenomenon, a record with a life entirely of its own.

In May I had asked my sister Hazel to pack in her job as a nursery manager and come and work with me. We had become a proper family business. I'd moved from my office of the last eleven years, the aforementioned living room floor, into a little serviced office in Queens Park, where we had the luxury of two telephone lines and a fax machine. Edwyn was more or less constantly away on tour or on promotional duty and I was so crazily busy I couldn't think straight. The fact that we owned the record outright was in many ways a brilliant thing, especially financially, but day-to-day it was a logistical nightmare, as it was being managed by the world's least-organised woman and her very organised but new to the game wee sister. I would sometimes turn to Hazel and see a look of disbelieving panic on her face. The phone never stopped ringing, whether in the office or back at the flat. We had licensed the record around the world, about eight deals in all, but we were the hub.

Our licensees would enthuse about the convenience of being able to call one number for the answer to all questions, rather than the usual layers of departments, but for Hazel and me, it was intensive stuff. At four o'clock, I would pick Will up from school and the little soul would have to amuse himself in our cramped office for a few hours until I could finally get him out of there, feed him something unsuitable, bath him, get him to bed and then get back on the phone to overseas time zones. As a naturally slothful person, this frenetic level of activity was a shock to my system.

I would also travel a lot with Edwyn, sometimes leaving William with Hazel and her partner Mark, but often taking him with me, in a way that would most definitely draw stern disapproval from the school authorities nowadays. But back then they were more relaxed and didn't argue with my theories about adventure and learning by experience, in spite of the obvious flimsiness of my excuses. But as far as we were concerned, William simply had to come with us; we would have missed him too much. He was a tremendously easy-going traveller, coping with jet lag much better than I and taking the harum-scarum schedule in his stride. Before he was seven he had been in all corners of the globe, but at that age I really think he believed that this was what everyone's dad did. I used to call him our icebreaker, as he bowled across the world, charming everyone who crossed his path. I'm sure he wishes he could repeat the adventure now he's grown up and that it was rather wasted on him as such a young kid.

·

EDWYN COPED MANFULLY with every piece of lunacy that real success throws at you, something we weren't accustomed to. We were no longer young or stupid or gullible, but it was still impossible to avoid completely mad sketches wherever you went.

I have a video of Edwyn in Athens, on Greece's most-watched TV show, an epic affair that ran for three hours of unremitting tackiness on a Sunday night. He managed to restrain the producer's determination to drape him in dancing women whilst he mimed to 'A Girl Like You', and kept at least a few feet between him and these scantily clad lovelies. However, he then re-appears to do his second number. Here, he strokes his chin quizzically as the fabulously pneumatic, blonde presenter delivers a long-winded, eyelash-batting introduction to camera. She is a gorgeous, sexy thing wearing a gold lamé dress and holding a golden gun, which turns out to be a fag lighter, 70s-style. Eventually she turns to Edwyn, leans on his shoulder and purrs: 'Edwyn ... you light my fire ...' and activates the fag lighter. At which Edwyn pulls a saucy face, Frankie Howerd style, nods and replies: 'Thanks very much!' Cue the music!

In Belgium, Edwyn appeared on the Flemish version of *Top of the Pops*, at number two in the charts. At number one was the country's favourite comedian, dressed up as a tree, singing a charming number about arborophilia, or tree fucking, as it is more commonly known. There really is such a thing, but in those pre-internet days, it was a pastime only popular in the Low Countries.

On arrival in the Philippines in the spring of 1996, the three of us were greeted by a phalanx of television cameras and microphones. They all walked backwards down the corridor to Arrivals, filming us as if we were Mick and Bianca Jagger in the 70s, except I'd just spilled a glass of champagne into my lap on the plane and looked like I'd wet myself. We were whisked through the diplomatic channel to a press conference where I annoyed our host, Bella Tan, record company supremo, Manila's top female gangster and genuine old mate of Imelda Marcos, by politely refusing to sit at the top table. (I'm the manager, not the attention seeker ... well, not in these circumstances anyway.) We were on the front page of the national paper the next day. Edwyn did eight TV shows in two days, where he was backed by a boy band, who wore trendy sports clothes and danced like N'Sync. Apparently, in the absence of Edwyn, these boys had been dancing to 'A Girl Like You' on every media outlet for months and the population strongly associated it with them. They were called The Universal Dancers, six of them, including my special favourites, the sixteen-year-old twins, James and Jim. Everywhere he went, Edwyn saw cash being exchanged in a blatant way. Old fashioned payola for TV and radio exposure was alive and well in Manila. We were warned to keep a close eye on William, on account of the local craze for kidnapping the children of people in the public eye and holding them for ransom. We'd only been there two days and I couldn't wait to leave.

At the end of this whirlwind tour, having fulfilled their requirements, we were unceremoniously dumped in the car park at the airport by one of our host's scar-faced honchos. Lovely. This is a country of some 95 million people and all of them watch TV like maniacs. Edwyn was a celebrity in the airport and on the plane out of there. But this was celebrity of the flimsiest variety. I guarantee if we'd gone back the following week, they would have had no clue as to who we were.

•

HALF WAY THROUGH 1996, and after almost two years of non-stop running, I decided that this last promotional tour of the Far East, encompassing nuttiness of every hue in Hong Kong, Japan, Korea, Taiwan, Singapore, Malaysia and last but not least, the delightful Philippines, should bring to an end the story of the crazy, wonderful record. I don't think either of us was cut out for the pop star lifestyle. We were so tired. I kept wondering how the properly famous do it. To keep going, they must really love and need the attention. No amount of attendant luxury could make up for the tyranny of the schedule or the inanity of the promotional and publicity activity. For us, this stuff was only bearable in small doses. I knew we would enjoy it all as hilarious memories and anecdotes, but I was so glad it was winding down. With our track record, I reckoned it was something we wouldn't be repeating any time soon.

•

EDWYN COULDN'T WAIT to get off the promo bus and back to the quiet of life in the studio. Seb had found our new studio, West Heath Studios in West Hampstead, in mid-1995. A beautiful old stabling block originally used for the Fire Brigade horses, it had been turned into a recording studio by a group of guys in the early 80s, one of whom was Alan Parsons, the Abbey Road engineer who recorded Pink Floyd's *Dark Side of the Moon*. It was the place of our dreams and we're still there. Hazel and I have our office there and Will feels as if he grew up in this building, as it was the place he'd come to when I picked him up from school each day.

My housekeeping has always been the laughing stock of all my friends, and by early 1996 things were truly falling apart – my laundry system in particular. This consisted of two giant piles on the kitchen floor. Clean pile and dirty pile. Will was fond of curling up for a nap in the clean pile. It got to the stage where I was too embarrassed to let the man in to read the meter. I had decided that between mad amounts of work, looking after Will and house cleaning something had to give, and skivvying it was. Edwyn would for years regale strangers with the hilarious story of how he set off on a tour of the US, leaving behind a half-drunk can of Red Stripe by his side of the bed. Apparently when he returned twelve weeks later it was still there. I'm sure he's right; I certainly didn't notice. In any case, I countered, it was he who had left it there, not me.

Around this time, Edwyn did an interview for *Q*, the major UK music magazine, where the journalist comes round, sits in your living room and checks out your record collection. I *did* tidy up for them, but nonetheless they were to write: 'Pop star Edwyn Collins lives in a hovel in Kensal Rise.' Very cheeky. In any case, my reasoning was that if I got my head down and concentrated on the work in hand, perhaps we would soon find an escape route from the 'hovel'. And so it proved to be.

•

IN JUNE 1996 we bought our house in Kilburn. It had been languishing on the market for a year because, in the language of the estate agent, it required extensive renovation. The roof was knackered, the plaster on the walls was soft and crumbly, there was evidence of dry rot and some of the ceilings were bulging downwards in a threatening manner. Obviously, the house for us.

Six months of home improvement drama later, we moved in, leaving behind the little flat I had called home for thirteen years. Since we had already acquired the studio, all of Edwyn's gear and most of his general junk had been moved there, allowing us to move into our new home with hardly any stuff. Three floors of virtual emptiness. On our first night there, we rattled around, three fish out of water. Will, aged six, was aware that he would finally have a bedroom to himself and had been excited about planning it. He had a brilliant platform bed, constructed by Pav, our good mate who had been the project manager on the rebuild. In the end, though, the actuality of sleeping in his own room, with us not only in a different room, but *on a different floor,* proved too much for Will, a child who had been used to having a parent within stretching distance his whole life: 'I hate this GREAT, BIG, WANKER HOUSE!' he sobbed. 'What you need are SMALL, LITTLE HOUSES!'

In February 2005, Edwyn turned forty-five years old, an elder statesman in music now. He was in an untroubled place in his career. He was still recording, but without pressure to hit the heights. For the last ten years he and Seb had been established at their studios in West Hampstead, where they had carved out a reputation for themselves and the studio as a unique environment to make records in. They had augmented the equipment there with an ever-expanding collection of vintage recording effects and microphones. They were both totally wedded to the place. At his ease, Edwyn had just completed the recording of a set of songs for a new album, a record which reflected his

Card system in
operation
6.30pm – 8.30 am
Mon – Fri
and all weekend

powers as an accomplished songwriter of huge experience. Edwyn was a sharp self-editor and his quality control was rigorous. This was a fine record and he was looking forward to moving to the mixing stage. Life was busy.

At home I was unaware of any serious signs of trouble on the horizon. Edwyn and I had been together for just over twenty years. I had been his manager for about a year longer than we had been a couple. William was happily approaching his fifteenth birthday, growing up bonkers, but in a very loveable way.

I was semi-aware of a certain irritability about Edwyn, a slight tendency towards increasing grumpiness. I also knew that he was having headaches. This we both put down to an increase in his drinking. He was always a rubbish drinker, what our friend and Edwyn's former guitar player Steve Skinner, a Yorkshireman, called a 'one-pot screamer'. It didn't suit Edwyn; he couldn't handle it, and he seemed to go from totally sober to dead drunk in the space of about five minutes. So I thought I knew what the trouble was. Go easy on the drink. But Edwyn won't be told. So he swallowed the Solpadeine and carried on.

Only in recent times has Edwyn revealed to me the extent of his anxieties at that time. He may have seen the storm clouds gathering. In an interview lately he described: 'a sense of foreboding, a sense of agitation'. I also had no clue as to the extent of the pain he was suffering. He had not been to see a doctor in over a decade and now his fear prevented him from doing so, or even telling me how bad he felt. Apparently he had a dread of discovering the cause of the pain. For me this knowledge comes – too late – as shafts of pure guilt. My fault, my job to read the signs, to protect my family.

But none of the signs were sufficient to register a warning of the cataclysm to come. And so life moved stealthily forward towards the unavoidable.

CRISIS

On the morning of Sunday, 20 February 2005, Edwyn brought me a bowl of miso soup in bed. We'd never had that for breakfast before, but I think he'd been rooting around for something to work on a mild hangover. We'd been at a party at Pav's, our previously mentioned interior designer and his wife Henri's house the evening before – good friends of ours who lived about ten minutes' drive away in Harlesden. All three of us had gone to the party, William being pals for most of his life with their daughter, Stella. I'd driven, so that we could bring with us a new addition to our lives, a two-week-old kitten that Will had found in the middle of our street the previous freezing Monday night. Edwyn and I were feeding this tiny wee thing, strangely named Giles by our son, with some special milk from the vet every four hours or so.

On the evening Will brought the kitten home, just after

we returned from the vet, I'd had a call from Seb at the studio, asking me to come and collect Edwyn, who wasn't feeling too great. He'd been sick and was feeling dizzy. He was sure it had been some dodgy chicken he'd had. Back home, he was sick again a couple of times before heading for bed. Next day, we talked about going to hospital to have him checked out, but the dizziness was passing and he decided the slight food poisoning diagnosis was probably right. And I left it at that.

At the party, the following Saturday night and six nights after the chicken incident, Edwyn appeared to be fine. A few glasses of wine later, I abandoned the car and we cabbed it home. Edwyn had gone fairly easy that night, as we were both on kitten duty.

And so, Sunday morning dawned and all seemed perfectly normal. On Sunday evening, around 6.30 pm, Edwyn was preparing dinner. He was the chef in our house (I'm more or less hopeless, and he had discovered a real passion for cooking, coincidently, not long after coming to live with me). That night we were having a hearty winter stew he had prepared the day before. I decided to go and collect the car, reckoning it would only take about twenty minutes. Edwyn agreed I should go as long as I meant twenty minutes and no longer. I picked up a minicab from the office round the corner and less than ten minutes later was driving homewards. I had considered calling in to say hi to Pav and Henri, but decided against it as Edwyn would certainly be annoyed if his dinner timing was messed about

with. So humdrum, so ordinary. Still no inkling. This journey, these minutes before, still replay in my mind. Our life
before, all that we assumed.

●

I WALKED THROUGH the door and smelt burning. The
potatoes had boiled dry on the stove. I moved through to
the kitchen and switched off the gas, calling, 'Edwyn, the
potatoes ...'

And then came the fear. It must have hit William too
because as I ran upstairs to the first-floor living room, the
room where we watched TV, I was calling Edwyn's name.
Not loudly, not panicky, but as I got there I saw Will had
beaten me to it, descending from our top-floor bedroom,
where he watched TV. Normally he would ignore our
shouting up and down the stairs. So his cry of alarm was
confirmation. Something was wrong.

Edwyn was on the floor in front of the sofa. I think
Antiques Roadshow was on in the background. An integral
part of a cosy Sunday night in, now we were old folks. His
body was contorted, the right side caught underneath him.
Will and I both flew to our knees beside him, uncoiling him.
We didn't panic or scream. Will got a pillow for his head.
He remembers me cradling his dad's head, kissing his face,
reassuring him. Edwyn's face was lopsided. He was semi-
conscious, trying to speak and unable to. He seemed scared.

The phone.

First, an ambulance. I was clear and detailed to the
woman on the switchboard: 'I think he's had a stroke.'

41

I had never seen one before, but this was my first thought. I described his symptoms quickly and accurately. I didn't freak out. I spoke quietly from outside on the landing, so as not to frighten Will or Edwyn. Then I called Hazel, across London in Islington. How long before the ambulance came? I have no idea. The pictures are strong in my memory, as are many of the things that were said. My thoughts are harder to recall and the timeline, the order of events, I know I get wrong.

•

IT COULDN'T HAVE been very long. There were two male paramedics, capable and kind. Taking readings, asking questions, writing results and some of my answers on their latex gloves. Edwyn is a tall man, six foot one, but wrapping him in a blanket, strapping him to a trolley and getting downstairs and into the ambulance seemed effortless to them. Before they arrived, Will was fretting about how we'd get his dad downstairs. One of the guys suggested to Will that he might want to take something with him to pass the time in hospital as there might be a lot of waiting around – a book or something. In his shocked state, Will took this as an instruction and on the journey to the Royal Free Hospital in Hampstead, he sat in the ambulance staring unseeingly at his Arsenal book. The recollection of this image still distresses me.

•

42

A QUICK JOURNEY, in spite of the speed bumps, which I really notice. Then Edwyn is in the resuscitation room and lots of things happen in a rush. Nobody pushes me out of the way. I'm allowed to be with him all the time. An A&E doctor takes a history. I see Edwyn's blood pressure monitored for the first time. I will become fixated on this very soon, but at this point I don't understand its significance, even when someone comments that it is very high. Lines go in. Edwyn throws up a few times. Another doctor comes, a neurologist or possibly a neurosurgeon, not senior. Edwyn is to have an immediate scan. While they are doing this, I try to find a place where I can get a good signal on my phone and call Hazel again, who is on her way, having dashed to the house to feed the kitten. I tell her we're in the Royal Free, fifteen minutes' drive away at this time on a Sunday night. She is already covering all the bases, as she will continue to do for many months. Giles the kitten will soon have a new home with her and then, when that becomes impractical, with Pav and Henri.

Then we are back again in resuscitation. The A&E doctor comes back with films from the scan and talks to both of us. I don't know if Edwyn can understand, but I think I'm glad the doctor assumes he can. He shows me the film and explains that Edwyn has had a large bleed inside his brain. He points out a white mass, which I recall as being roughly centrally located. He tells me a neurologist will be coming to talk to me very soon. He will be able to tell us more. I start to ask questions, which he gently sidesteps, explaining that it's not his field of expertise. We then have our first moment of absurdity. He asks: 'It is the Edwyn Collins I think it is?'

'I think so, well, I only know one,' I say.

'I just answered a question about you in a pub quiz the other night.' And he and Edwyn laugh a little.

Does he get it?

•

SOON AFTER THIS William goes very white and almost faints. It's shock. They put him on a trolley and I get him a Coke and a bar of chocolate, not to spoil him, but because the nurses tell me he needs a blood sugar boost.

I call Edwyn's sister in Glasgow. Petra, eighteen months younger than Edwyn and devoted acolyte since childhood. At this time an advocate, the Scottish equivalent of a barrister, now a judge, never a panicker, she decides to wait until morning to tell Edwyn's mum. They can't travel until then and at least one of them will have had some sleep. I promise to call back when I know more. The impact of these calls is something I only consider much later.

Hazel arrives. Thank God. I need her, Will needs her.

•

THE NEUROLOGIST TAKES me alone into a side room. What he tells me I absorb silently. And this is what I feel. An explosion. My blood, surging. My skin tingling, pins and needles. My eyes feel like they don't fit.

44

Edwyn is perilously ill. He may die. A blood vessel in his brain has burst under pressure. It has trailed a path of destroyed tissue in its wake, continuing until the pressure itself stopped the bleeding. However, the mass of compressed blood threatens further damage and the risk of the bleeding resuming is high. If this happens, the outcome will be catastrophic. He will almost certainly die. The neurologist goes on to say, bizarrely, as if it comforts, that should this happen Edwyn will be unconscious and feel nothing. And he suggests that I gather anyone who needs to be here as soon as possible. He says these words in a gentle, practised manner. There is absolutely nothing nasty about this man, whom I will never see again. But I still feel a kind of hatred towards him.

I must have asked him something, because it is around this time that I start to think of Wednesday as a target. Stay alive until Wednesday. You must stay alive until Wednesday, my love. Stay alive.

•

I WANT TO stop time dead in its tracks. I want to rewind and fix everything. Take us back. I'll fix it. This isn't a fleeting thought, it's a constant yearning, for many months. Sometimes I daydream that it's possible, like rewriting a story. With the realisation that it can't be done, I double up in despair.

•

WE ARE MOVED upstairs to a ward. Hazel takes Will home to our house. Edwyn slips fitfully in and out of a troubled sleep state. For the first night, there is, fortuitously, a male staff nurse who is experienced in neurology. He examines Edwyn and takes his blood pressure every hour.

The middle of that first night, about four in the morning, I ask the nurse if I can step outside and make a call. He says of course, but I must tell him if I am going to leave Edwyn's side. He can't be left alone. Out in the lift bay, I give in to my fear and call my younger sister, Nan, in Glasgow, a nurse and ward manager of almost thirty years. I wanted to wait until morning but I can't bear it. I want to talk to her desperately. By six in the morning she's at the airport, trying to get on the first flight.

Daylight dawns and the hospital stirs to life. I sit dumbly by Edwyn's side, watching him, unchanged. After breakfast (not for Edwyn, he is nil by mouth, attached to a drip for hydration), Nan arrives. Hazel brings Will and then, in the afternoon, Edwyn's mum, Myra, and Petra. Hazel drives me home for an hour to have a quick bath and change my clothes. I feel grotty. Being at the house while Edwyn lies in hospital is a mind-bending torment. We speed back again.

In the evening we are transferred across the hallway to another ward. I don't know why, bed pressure perhaps. We say goodnight to everyone else, who head for home, and Nan and I settle down for the second night's vigil. Having been told by the excellent nurse of the night before not to

46

leave him, we don't ask permission to stay, fearful that it won't be given.

Hospitals have something called receiving wards, a sort of no-man's-land you are sent to while you jostle for a bed in the specialist unit you ought to be in. These places seem to occupy the lowest position in the hospital pecking order. Nobody wants to be there and nobody wants to work there. Doctors appear to be in a super rush to get out as quickly as possible and the nursing care makes you shudder. Horrendous. This is where we washed up for the next few days of Edwyn's hospital ordeal. The exception to the rule as far as the bad nursing was concerned is Richard, a nurse who visits in the early morning. He is a member of the critical care outreach team, a senior charge nurse, and explains that his team will keep Edwyn under supervision in case he needs help with his breathing. That's how he puts it, and the significance eludes me in my scrambled state. Looking back, I realise the expectation that Edwyn would crash was there from the start.

·

Wednesday is a red herring. By the time it has come and gone we have watched Edwyn wrestle for his life, amid a confusion of neglect and uselessness, for three days.

Bizarrely, there is no treatment for stroke other than paracetamol. To reduce Edwyn's blood pressure, which is horribly high, would be to risk further bleeding. Conversely, to leave the pressure this high presents an equal risk. So the protocol is to do nothing for three days and then introduce the drugs to bring it down very slowly. It's a stomach-knotting balancing act. Meanwhile he lies, experiencing a cerebral irritation which makes him attempt to launch himself from his bed every few minutes. He is seized with an involuntary lurch to the left-hand side. If he wasn't caught, he would be on the floor each time these wild flights happen, which seems like a hundred times a day.

We are with him day and night: in the long hours of semi-darkness, during the day under the unremitting harshness of the strip lighting. Hours of lying underneath these things would drive you nuts at the best of times. For Edwyn it's actually painful. I know this because when the lights finally go off he is a bit more settled. But the night shifts are an especial ordeal. The staff resent our continuous presence. There are old people around us, some distressed, some demented. A few of the staff actually shout at them. A nurse starts an argument with me in the middle of the night. For some reason, she interprets our vigil as a personal slight, our being there at all times an insult to her professionalism. I don't care, I will not leave him. At one point staff claim to have completed full neurological observations more often than we ever saw. Nan, with her wealth of experience, watches like a hawk, and deals with the hard-hearted incompetents that run this miserable ward with the cold fury they deserve.

•

ON WEDNESDAY AFTERNOON, in a state of exhaustion as he is unable to get any restful sleep in this strange state of restless semi-consciousness he is experiencing, Edwyn is moved to the calm and care of the stroke unit, where the first dose of anti-hypertensive medication is given. It doesn't even graze the blood pressure. One of the ward sisters, Marion, a very caring nurse, mutters her concern. The knot in my stomach tightens. Edwyn passes a swallow test, is no longer 'nil by mouth' and is given his first drink of water in three days. He has six cups in quick succession, like a man who has been in the desert, ignoring all pleas to sip it slowly. So, while they were posturing about their professionalism on that hateful ward, Edwyn was dehydrating.

I go home for a change of clothes only to discover that some newspaper people, the *Sun* and others, have been at our door. There must be some means by which they sniff out bad news, although I'm surprised they are interested. Edwyn's not mainstream enough to excite any interest from the celebrity end of journalism. It appears they don't know very much, just rumour, but I decide that in order to short-circuit any false information, I will put a short statement on his website and release it through our agent and close friend, Russell Warby, to the music magazine, *NME*: 'Edwyn suffered a cerebral haemorrhage on Sunday night. He is being well-looked after in hospital. When there is more to tell, I'll let you know.'

•

ON THURSDAY NIGHT, Nan sends me home. Edwyn is now in a room on his own. We have met a nurse called Sarah who works nights in the stroke unit. Very experienced and confidence inspiring, Edwyn will come to know her well in the weeks and months to come. Sarah expresses quiet concern about the ongoing crazy level of Edwyn's blood pressure, which rarely deviates from the 250/150 level (the normal blood pressure for a man Edwyn's age is around 130/80). But this is how it has been all week. Hopefully as they introduce more medication it will slowly reduce. Nan tells me to give both Edwyn and her some peace and go get some sleep. When I arrive home, Will is going through the reams of goodwill messages on Edwyn's website with Granny Myra and Petra. We all take comfort from the warmth of the words and genuine shock and concern of these good people who have been up until now very quiet participants in his music. Edwyn's fans aren't a showy bunch. But many of them are stepping forward now to offer at times awkward but always touchingly sincere words of comfort. We go to bed feeling a little more positive.

●

NAN SPENDS THE early hours of Friday morning alone with Edwyn. When I turn up at dawn, she tells me he has had a more peaceful night and that at one point he even sang to her. She couldn't distinguish the words and didn't recognise the song, but it was a moment of tranquillity they shared.

I send her off home for a sleep.

Around eight o'clock I call a nurse to check Edwyn's pupils. I have a neurotic notion that he's less responsive. She thinks he's okay. Myra and Petra join me and he has a visit from the consultant neurologist who tells us that his age and this type of haemorrhagic stroke, if you survive it, bode for a better recovery than the other type, caused by a clot.

Less than thirty minutes later, at around 11 am, Edwyn is in a coma.

COPING

WE THREE HAVE gone for a quick cup of coffee downstairs as Edwyn's nurse wants to give him a wash and a shave. He seems asleep as we leave. As she tends to him she becomes concerned. His pupils are non-reactive. He is bleeding again, deep inside.

We arrive back on the ward amid a flurry of activity. Here is the strangest thing: we barely utter a sound, even when the doctor on duty tells us Edwyn has taken a turn for the worse. His breathing, through an orange-coloured tube in his airway, is more laboured with every try. As we wait for the crash team to arrive, we stand mutely around him, his mother, his sister, me. We're frozen to the spot with terror. I actually feel frightened of Edwyn himself; it's as if he's transformed into something so alien, so fearful. I'm watching him fall into a place I can't follow. None of us touch him.

The crash team arrives with a trolley loaded with equipment. The senior member introduces herself briefly and clearly. Her name is Maggie and she explains that Edwyn will be placed on a ventilator to take over his breathing, that he will become a patient of the intensive care unit. That when the machine is in place he will have a scan to determine what specifically has happened. I catch my first glimpse of a member of the team who will later become a touchstone for Edwyn, a rather severe-looking girl with dark hair and glasses. As we are ushered away by the stroke unit doctors, a controlled hive of activity begins, and I feel an increasing sense of Edwyn slipping beyond my reach.

We spend the next hour and more huddled together on the plastic chairs by the lifts, outside the ward, waiting. My boy arrives with his Auntie Nan. When I called her he was asleep, but they made it to the mini cab office round the corner in minutes. During the journey they held on to each other and didn't speak. I get down on the floor with him (there aren't enough chairs), and put his head on my lap. Hazel is on her way to King's Cross Station where she is due to collect my brother, David, arriving from Scotland. I've spoken to her and she in turn to David. The affect of these exchanges has to be borne alone until they meet. Meanwhile our wait continues. People approach, concerned, ask if we are all right? We break the tension with occasional murmurs of comfort to each other. It's a long time. What's happening? We don't dare ask.

•

AT LAST THE doctor emerges to tell us that after some difficulty, Edwyn has been ventilated. The machine is now breathing for him. He's going to be taken for the scan that will reveal the extent of the damage. The medical people around us say very little, their expressions are so grave we have nothing to cling to. One of the doctors exchanges some gentle words with Will. They suggest we go downstairs to the cafeteria for the forty minutes or so that it will take before they can give us more definitive information. And so we obey.

As we exit the lift on the ground floor, I stay back a few yards and quietly say to Nan, out of earshot of the others, 'I think he's gone...'

'Maybe, love,' she answers softly. 'Let's just take things one step at a time.'

Nan understands the significance of all that has occurred and so do I. I reach out for hope, for positive thoughts, but I'm flooded with dread.

•

OUR STEPS LEAD us through the thronging crowds of a Friday lunchtime in search of a place to pass these minutes. The cafeteria is full to bursting, there's nowhere to go. We can't possibly leave the hospital, it doesn't even occur to us, so we end up huddled by the lifts again. I go to the shop to get Will a drink and a bar of chocolate. I stand in a queue, and I remember clearly thinking how strange this is, there is nothing to distinguish me from all these people. I'm in this

55

⁻queue and where is Edwyn? What is happening to him right now? Where will he go next? Then I remember I'm in a hospital. This happens here, every day, all the time. Multiple horrors. I'm not sure I can relate the weird stuff that flashed through my mind at this time. Unnamed, surreal awfulness. And thoughts of life without Edwyn, as I stand in a queue in a hospital shop. Reality fading in and out.

•

PERHAPS BECAUSE HE is an only child, William has always been a very family-minded boy, close to and fond of all grandparents, aunts, uncles and cousins. At this horrible time he found himself enveloped in family love and concern, everyone distracting themselves from their own thoughts by looking out for him. Petra is very wise and suggests that we wait for David and Hazel to arrive from the station before we go back upstairs.

'Will is going to need his Uncle David,' she suggests. I know Petra is feeling the dread too. Will is surrounded by women and David is a strong and loving male presence in his life. Petra is right, and strangely, we feel no urgency.

It is a great relief when they arrive, to be all together, a little safety in our swelling numbers. The journey to the hospital and finding a blasted parking space has seemed unending. Nan waits by the hospital door to meet them. Hazel, who has worked with Edwyn and me for fourteen years, is in pieces. She takes a moment to compose herself before we are united, a great gang of us by the lifts. And now we have to get back among the crowds waiting to rush the first open lift door, to take us up to the waiting news. We made these moves, I know we did, but my memories are indistinct. I was engulfed by terror and for a time lost touch with my surroundings. The next thing I'm aware of is a doctor talking to Petra, Will and me.

But then the first of many miracles occurs.

The doctor doesn't say the words I am dreading. Instead, he speaks hurriedly and quietly, and tells us that the neurosurgeons who have examined the scans want to try to save Edwyn by operating to evacuate the bleed. This was the term he used; I remember the oddness of it, vividly. He goes on to explain that they need to get the go-ahead from their boss, the consultant, and that Edwyn is being prepared for the surgery right now in the intensive care unit. We should go there.

Will has a bad reaction to this news. He's calling out, 'No, no, Dad, no.' He's very frightened that they have to operate on his dad. I try to reassure him that this is good news, they are going to help him, but all is confusion for poor Will at this time. I am dizzy with relief, fresh hope suddenly surging through me.

We pile into another lift, to the fourth floor, and find Maggie the ward's sister at the entrance to the intensive care unit. She confirms that the go-ahead has been given and Edwyn is about to be transferred to surgery. Indeed, in the background I can see a number of people in theatre scrubs bustling around a bed. Moments later we clear the way as Edwyn is pushed past us, lost in a sea of paraphernalia, leaving me again frozen and unable to physically reach for him. I'm so afraid of this strange entity he has become. A medical emergency. The contrast between our reactions – paralysed fear, confusion, helplessness and sense of unreality, and the swift, practised calm of the staff for whom this is commonplace, is marked. I feel we inhabit different planets. I'm in awe of them.

•

AGAIN THERE IS nothing for us to do. Will is begging to go home, to escape. So we decide that that is the best thing to do. Our home is a short drive away, and there is nowhere for us even to sit in peace in hospital. It will be some hours before Edwyn emerges from surgery. At this point I detach. I can't think about what is happening to him, how dangerous it is. Petra has exactly the right idea. I'm not sure when she started saying it, but with each move we make, each revelation, she would say firmly, 'Right. Next step.'

•

I REMEMBER LITTLE or nothing of those intervening hours at home. I know I heard that my mum was on her way from Scotland, anxiously leaving my step-dad, Jim, behind. He is still recovering from a leg amputation eight months previously. I'm the oldest of four children. Grace, Nan, David and Hazel. This will become one of Edwyn's early speech mantras as he tries to pin down his memories of familiar words. Over and over again, listing our names, in various orders.

When my wise and funny, gentle, wry, family-loving dad, William Maxwell, was forty-seven years old, he died of a brain tumour. He collapsed at work and, after a five month struggle, we lost him. This was in 1977, when I was nineteen and my youngest sister Hazel only eleven. Thirty years later, the pain of loss is much less, but the missing him goes on. On the interminable train journey south that day to be by my side and complete the family around me, the memories for Mum are strong and the pain lived afresh.

•

WE RETURN TO the hospital around 5 pm. Will doesn't want to come and we all understand why. He has gone into a world of his own, self-preservation, away from shock upon shock. He goes to a drama group for teenagers on Friday nights at our local theatre, the Tricycle. They are in the middle of rehearsals for the big production of the year, due in a few weeks. He decides to go as usual. The only way for him to cope right now is to pretend as hard as he can that it's not happening.

But his dad has made it through this part of the ordeal, safe and sound. Ridiculous as it may be, and especially in the light of discoveries I would later make, it never occurred to me that he wouldn't. As soon as they told me that they would operate, that he was still alive, that he had a chance, it was as if I had gone into suspended animation for the duration of the surgery. Don't think. Just hang on.

Next step.

•

MY FIRST IMPRESSIONS of the intensive care unit are that Edwyn is in a place of safety, enveloped in skill, constantly watched over. In the midst of fear and dread, this is a relief. When we arrive he is still undergoing the many procedures to settle and establish him in the unit, and we have to wait a while longer before we can see him. A brief glimpse of an indistinct figure in the distance through a window in the locked doors tells me that Edwyn is real, he still exists. We sit in the purgatory of the relatives' room, waiting for the summons. To gain access to the ward you have to lift a telephone receiver and ask permission, usually given, and have the doors buzzed open. Two visitors at a time.

Myra and I are the first to go through the doors, where the ICU rules are explained. No outdoor clothes. Plastic apron on and hands washed with antibacterial scrub. We observe this ritual solemnly and obediently. I'm sure Myra has joined me in this Twilight Zone. We are introduced to Sinead, Edwyn's dedicated, one-to-one nurse. She is Irish and, you can't help but notice, very beautiful. Amazing green eyes.

And finally, here is Edwyn. He is in a semi propped-up position, although deeply unconscious. He is medically sedated. He has no clothes on his top half. I remember the absurdity of Sinead apologising for having cut his T-shirt before he was taken to surgery. His head is swathed in bandages, with some writing on the left side. 'No bone flap.' I register a blip of curiosity about this. My curiosity instinct is kicking in, a good thing in theory, but will soon grow to mammoth proportions and become a source of torment. I will need to know everything and will never know enough.

As you would expect, there is lots of technical equipment and quite a bit of noise. Edwyn has a tube in his open mouth with a big tap-like ending on it, connecting him to the ventilator. Sinead never stops working; Edwyn's gear needs total attention. Alarms go off constantly, heart-stopping at first, until you realise it just means something needs changing, resetting, a refill attaching. Nothing to panic about. After each procedure, adjustment, reading, observation, Sinead turns to Edwyn's chart, a thing the size of a wall map – a new one for every day – and makes a record. Now, this is how mental I am that day. Before I even hold Edwyn's hand or think about muttering some words to his unresponsive being, I look for the monitor that will tell me his blood pressure reading. I find it quickly and register relief as a physical adrenalin rush. It looks entirely normal. Sinead sees me looking at the monitor and points to a white liquid substance that enters Edwyn's body via a thin tube.

'That's the good stuff,' she smiles.

And I look at his face.

In the coming weeks and months there will be so much more anxiety and worry, but for this moment I am transported to a place of happiness, as I see in Edwyn's face that the horrible pain and pressure of the last week, which manifested itself in a strained, puffy, desperate appearance, has completely evaporated. Indeed, gazing at him, I don't believe I have seen his expression so relaxed and restful for many months. Whatever work these demigods, the surgeons, had performed, they had given him, for the time being, an ease that his poor body and brain so needed. I was thankful.

Nan later tells of her amazement when Sinead is completing her neuro-observations, which involve checking the reactions of Edwyn's pupils. As Sinead checks, each pupil contracts in turn under the light of her torch. Incredible signs of brain activity.

•

WE TAKE TURNS to be with him, myself, Myra, Petra and Nan. We have all of us begun a process that will continue for months, that of expecting Sister Ramsay (Nan) to be able to answer all our questions, to be the fount of all knowledge, our personal expert – a role she fulfils slightly reluctantly, and always cautiously. She walks a tightrope of translating for us and helping us understand as much as possible, which is very comforting, but is careful not to speculate on things that are beyond her field of expertise, or tread on the toes of those whose care Edwyn is under. Unless they deserve it: ever the professional, but this time it's personal. For Myra, Petra and myself she is an especial crutch. I don't know how I'd have got through these times without her steady, reassuring back up.

.

DR CHAKROBARTI IS impossibly young, but extremely serious, and one of the neurosurgeons who operated on Edwyn. We have to wait for a meeting that evening with him for the full picture of how Edwyn is doing. In later weeks when I see him in the lifts or by Edwyn's bed, in a much lighter mood, beaming at Edwyn, he will appear to have an aura of brilliance around him. Imagine being his mum, I would think; how ridiculously proud she must be.

His manner is quiet, sober and frank. Everything you want, really, except I'm hoping against hope that all his words will be encouraging. This turns out not to be the case. The first thing he does is ask us how much we understand about what has happened to Edwyn up until his collapse this morning. I briefly run through the events of recent days as best as I have understood them. He nods and proceeds to explain the nature of the surgery he and his colleagues have performed and what the immediate dangers are.

'Edwyn remains dangerously ill,' he begins, and immediately we are all back in the grip of fear.

The greatest risk, he explains, is of swelling occurring post-operatively. He warns that if this happens, Edwyn will probably die. He doesn't flinch from using the word. It's

63

crazy, but I wish he would lie. He does say, and I remember this, that the risk of bleeding recurring is slight, again triggering the vague ping of wonder in me. That danger has passed?

He goes on to explain the likely long-term effects of the bleeds in Edwyn's brain. He counsels that, on the evidence of what they witnessed during surgery, the damage is likely to be severe. Petra asks if he means both mental and physical? He nods a quiet assent, then asks if there is anything we want to ask him.

Later there are so many questions, but for now there are just a basic few. I ask if there is a timeframe for the danger. How many days?

'The next three or four.' That's clear, then. The target. Beyond, we will deal with. Next step.

Myra, who has already chosen the path of complete faith in the professionals who are watching over Edwyn, in combination with relentless positive thinking, emphasises her certainty that Edwyn is in the right place, a good place. And we set our course for the vigil ahead.

•

WHERE IS EDWYN in all of this? I'm recounting the experience of his illness mainly from the perspective of my own take on what happened. Edwyn, blessedly, has no memory of the acute phase. He has also lost approximately two weeks prior to the onset of events. From close questioning, I estimate Edwyn's awareness and memory beginning to return in a woolly way around five weeks from that first Sunday night. I say 'blessedly' because we believe his suffering was considerable before the second haemorrhage took him to pain-free oblivion. Eventually he would ask me to recount the whole story, chapter and verse, as he listened in silent amazement. But that was many months away. So, no memory, but something else. In a piece of writing he dictated to me in late 2006 for his internet blog, he unexpectedly said this: 'Little by little I experience new ways of life. For example I think I experienced death. I fought back to life. Confusing and generally surreal.'

I asked him to tell me more. He was lost in thought for a while.

'I remember, I don't remember, but a feeling.'

Then, 'I think so.'

That's all I got.

•

AT TIMES LIKE these for people like me – the faithless, the irreligious – strange things happen. I didn't start believing in higher powers, but I did pray. Or maybe I just pleaded. I'd reach for my dad, for Edwyn's grandfather, and beg them to help. I had a dozen little superstitious tics that I shared with no-one, and that I carried with me for many months. When people wrote and told me they were praying, lighting candles, organising something called remote healing, for God's sake, I was desperately grateful. I'd take anything. One couple wrote to tell me that they kept a picture of Edwyn in their living room and would touch it for luck each time they passed. Another guy wrote that at times when all was quiet he would hear a chant start up in his head: 'Come on Edwyn, come on Edwyn ...'

But ultimately, that Friday night after his operation, and on subsequent nights, I knew that this was Edwyn's private battle and that his survival, having been made possible by the genius of modern neurosurgery, was now down to some struggle he was waging on a plane that we are not privy to as conscious humans. But (and feel free to scoff, and as a practised cynic I would too), I had a strong sense of this fight taking place, and also of my own helplessness to influence the outcome. Still, of this I was certain: if he did come back it would be to a life worth fighting for. If he couldn't continue to be Edwyn in a way that made sense to him, he would let go. Why did I absolutely know this? I did. I just did.

But I didn't yet know what the outcome would be. The first night we would not spend by his side, ironically, was the one where he was in the most danger, and under deep sedation. The hospital said we could phone and check on his progress through the night, and when the staff told us to go home we obeyed, which we hadn't done previously. Gazing at Edwyn, I knew I could leave him deep inside his silent struggle. It was time to retreat for a few hours, and allow myself to regroup. This is a measure of how much confidence you can have in the ICU; at least in our experience of it. The NHS at its brilliant best. No slacking, no lapses, the cutting edge. Everything here happened at such a level as to render my interference ludicrous.

·

WE GO BACK to the house. Mum arrives. I'm straight away back to being her child. She tells me she saw something in my face she recognised from her own life, something she hoped never to see on any of her children.

I have a glass of red wine. I'm craving it, a drink, suddenly. There is a tiny bit of exhilaration in the midst of the worry. He didn't die, he's still here, he will keep fighting. He didn't die.

We try to get some sleep.

Uncle David sleeps in beside Will. Hazel takes Mum over to her house. Nan gets in with me. How often can you phone without being a crazed nuisance? Several times during that night, as I pestered Nan, she judged it would be all right to call. Each time with the same result. No change. Stable. Temporary relief, respite. At one point I creep downstairs to let Myra know her son is holding his own.

·

THE NEXT MORNING we take turns to sit with Edwyn. We change shifts. We visit the public cafeteria for the endless cups of pretend cappuccino. They don't sell much: pre-packed sandwiches, canned drinks, chocolate biscuits. Later, as long-term residents, we will be admitted to the inner sanctum of the staff canteen. Let joy be unconfined.

Since that first Sunday night I find that I am sometimes thirsty, but never hungry. And never tired. For the time being, sleep and food are surplus to requirements. I do sleep, but never for long and I don't miss it. Amazing. I am totally wired, on red alert, watchful.

Throughout this long Saturday, Edwyn remains cocooned in his chemically-induced sleep. The sedation is like switching him to stand by, helping to reduce the risk of dangerous swelling in his brain. The 'No bone flap' message on his bandage means exactly that. Edwyn has had a cran- iotomy, which means a piece of skull has been removed. It is fairly sizeable and will allow his brain to do a little post- operative swelling without creating dangerous pressure.

But the doctors want to reduce the sedation as soon as they can, to see if Edywn returns to consciousness of his own volition. And if he does so safely. After an evening consultation with another of his neurosurgeons, again an implausibly young-looking man, called Dr Ahmed, we learn that an attempt will be made to wake him up tomorrow. Sitting beside him that evening, I hear Sinead, who talks away to him all the time as she goes about her tending care, say, 'Ah, come on Edwyn. Wake up for us ...' She's only known him for twenty-four hours, totally spark out, but she's rooting for him. It's got to be done, this waking, I know, but nonetheless, here we are again, seizing up with anxiety. There are bad things that can be revealed during this time. The first question is, Will he wake up?

Okay. Next step.

•

DAVID DRIVES MY car to the hospital after a night that is a carbon copy of the one before. Several middle-of-the-night calls to his nurse, a young man called Abraham whom I never meet in the flesh. I can't believe it's only a week since Edwyn's collapse.

Astonishingly, when we arrive at the hospital, the process of bringing him back to the land of the living has already begun. David, who has so far been part of the incredible back-room support team, in charge of logistics and transportation, is seeing Edwyn for the first time. I can see how affected he is, tears in his eyes as he absorbs the sight of his brother-in-law and friend – intubated, unconscious, attached to an array of monitors.

Soon we are watching with our hearts in our mouths, listening as Edwyn's nurse, a new one, a Kiwi girl, Emma, cajoles him to open his eyes. She calls his name and rubs her knuckles quite firmly into his upper chest. This will irritate Edwyn awake apparently; I'm a little worried his eyes will fly open and he'll punch her.

But it works, and lo, he languidly opens his eyes, which immediately roll up into his head. He tries to steady them. I'm holding his hand and grinning like an idiot, softly jabbering incomprehensible drivel at the poor soul. I squeeze his left hand and feel him reassuringly squeeze back. He's barely there, but he recognises us, he tries to smile with his eyes, the huge breathing tube in his mouth getting in the way of anything else. Imagine this awakening, how on earth must it have felt? But, amid the emotion, we all do our best to reassure, to soothe, because we know he can feel it. Even in the depths of this surreal, soupy world he inhabits. Back to sleep he goes.

But his new nurse doesn't let him rest for long. Just as they do when you come out of anaesthesia, she keeps jerking him back to the world and encourages us to do the same. It seems cruel; all he wants to do is close his eyes. I now know how hard it must have been to open them. Edwyn had double vision for many weeks after his reawakening. Months down the line he had to cover his left eye with his hand in order to focus. His balance mechanisms were non-existent. The mere act of opening his eyes for more than a few seconds to begin with would induce horrendous vertigo. Almost immediately his eyes would roll up in their sockets and he would be forced to close them, especially against the unrelenting harshness of the ever-present strip lighting. So he did really well in those first hours to get the message of recognition across to us.

•

I HAD FORMED a close relationship with one of the pieces of equipment Edwyn was hooked up to. He had a probe in his head attached to a monitor which measured something called intracranial pressure (which goes by the acronym ICP), or swelling, to you and me. Anything between 1 and 15 was fine. Above that, you start to worry. How did I know this? I must have winkled it out of someone during the last thirty-six hours. I am a pain in the neck.

I would sit for hours looking at my precious numbers, as if taking my eyes off them would somehow be tempting Fate. I don't really recommend this approach as eventually it drives you nuts, but there was nothing I could do to tame my obsession with the stats.

Until he woke up, Edwyn's ICP bumped along quietly at around 8, 9, 10. What would it do now? As the day wore steadily on and as Edwyn became easier to rouse, so the numbers inexorably climbed. I sat by his bedside around four o'clock in the afternoon, my teeth clenched, chest tight, watching the monitor hit its all-time high of 24. Blood pressure was back up again too. Weird spikes. Nobody seemed to be panicking except me. I wasn't causing a fuss, just having an internal, silent panic. Then, gradually, down came the ICP. Sean, the dashing charge nurse of the ICU, explained that that was what to expect after sedation: a surge of pressure, then if all is well, a slow decrease back to normal levels. All is well. An adjustment of the level of the infusion of anti-hypertensive (for the blood pressure), and my jaw begins to relax. I'm aware that my neck is sore. I think I've been holding my shoulders up around my ears for a week. Sean is just the type of person you need in a place like this, at times like these. Clever, immensely capable and always happy to talk to you. I could never convey how reassuring people like Sean and Sinead are through these days. They got me through the intolerable. I will never forget.

•

I'VE NOT FINISHED worrying, I'm afraid. It's too much, this day. I can't go home. Even though it's frowned upon, nobody objects when David and I bunk down to spend the night in the relatives room. I'm determined not to be a nuisance to his night nurse, an Aussie agency nurse who has never worked here before. But in my new role as a self-appointed ICU expert, I quietly keep an eye on things – good grief, does my egomania know no bounds? I can imagine Edwyn's reaction if he was in any fit state. A few years back, during a slow evening at the studio, Edwyn and Seb devised an idea for a great new TV programme called *Grace Knows Everything*. Grace sits in a swivel chair, rather like the one on *Mastermind*, except she takes questions from the audience. Any subject, she has an opinion and goes on at length until eventually a voiceover announces: 'I'm sorry, folks, we have to leave *Grace Knows Everything* here, as we have run out of time.' And so, the insufferable bore that is Grace is cut off in mid flow. The sad thing is, I didn't even take offence at their mocking. It was a bit too accurate.

•

APART FROM A sharp dip in Edwyn's blood pressure necessitating another adjustment during the night, the next day dawns with no further incident. This blood pressure rollercoaster is just beginning; I need to get used to it.

•

As DAWN BREAKS on Monday morning, 27 February, we are joined in the relatives' room by a couple of patient visitors. They are Asian, I think Bangladeshi. I remember a young girl, very stylish, very distressed. They are joined by two police officers who are comforting her. The girl's young brother has just been admitted from surgery to ICU following a car accident. His bed is placed next to Edwyn's and he is very poorly.

This is one of the hard things about ICU. There is a constant drama being played out in the relatives' room. There is no privacy; we are all caught up in a shared maelstrom. Some, like us, and this young lad's family, are too gripped in their own fear and terror to hold conversations with others about the state of the person who lies through the locked doors of the ward. So you are eyed curiously by the other group, who share the gory details of their family circumstances and keep each other updated with progress reports. I'm not the only deluded know-all around here. The place is full of experts, not just on their own family member, but on everyone else's. There is a lot of heated debate on what might be the best course of action for each patient. Amazing. Up to a point this behaviour is understandable. Some have been here weeks. But, reluctant as I am to have a go at anyone who finds themself in this stressful situation, there are a few competitive types among them. One mad woman would *brag* about her daft son who, having come off his motorbike seriously for the second time, was about to move out of the unit, having, happily, emerged from a two-week coma. 'We've just had the adaptations taken out of the house from the last time!' she gleefully shrieks. And his biker mates regaling anyone who would listen with their hilarious near-death bike crash stories.

And then there are the endless complaints about the ICU staff. Each member of staff is taken in turn, weighed in the balance and found wanting. Perhaps our experience of this unit is uniquely good, but I doubt it. And I certainly have no illusions about the patchiness of standards in the health service. We'll have plenty of experience of that in the months to come. But the good souls who worked in this unit did not deserve the damning gossip of the relatives' room. Sometimes it was easier to sit in the corridor.

Monday turns out to be a hectic day. On one of my early visits in to see Edwyn I get a shock. Where's my favourite number gone? The ICP number is nowhere to be seen. Sean quickly reassures me. The probe has gone too, as the danger of Edwyn's brain swelling is judged to have passed. No need to monitor it any more.

I'm torn between jumping up and down and a powerful feeling of disbelief. But Edwyn has come through this phase with absolute flying colours. The doctors, not for the last time, talk to me about how good his underlying health is. How strong he is. Looking at the state the poor man is in, this might seem to stretch the truth, but it's all relative. I agree wholeheartedly; I can feel the force of a fight from him, an inaudible vibration.

Will comes to see him today. This time Edwyn seems

upset. I'm worried he thinks I've made a mistake exposing his boy to the spectacle of his dad in these frightening surroundings. Will is subdued – fine with his dad, but clearly shaken by all he's had to cope with.

•

THE DAYS OF anxiety are far from over. There will be times I'm very scared that Edwyn might go properly backwards. But he never really does. All there is to do now is wait and watch as the truth about what has happened to Edwyn unfolds.

First of all, there is to be another operation. A consultant anaesthetist, very well groomed with bright lipstick and expensive jewellery, explains the risks and the benefits of a tracheostomy. Edwyn will need breathing support for some time to come and the awkwardness of the tube in his mouth is plainly obvious. I've already been asked to keep a close eye on his wayward left hand, which has had several goes at yanking his breathing tube out. His nurse explained that it's very precious, as putting it in proved very tricky. He had to have a woman's size tube in the end.

The tracheostomy is an alternative route for a breathing tube, through the trachea, or windpipe, and involves making an incision in the throat. Once sorted, it will make him much more comfortable and hopefully, in time, allow him to speak by means of a valve that will open and close to divert air to his vocal chords. There are risks apparently, but I have blotted them out. They must have been the usual

75

ones associated with anaesthesia needed during the operation. To dwell on them is not helpful. It seems clear that this procedure is vital. I sign the forms and the surgery is scheduled for Tuesday's list.

As we leave on Monday evening, the family of the young boy in the bed next to Edwyn are gathered in numbers that way exceed the rules of the ICU. But nobody seems to mind. The curtains are gathered round, bulging with so many people that they brush against Edwyn's bed, which upsets Myra a great deal, as do the sounds of crying and praying that fill the ward. I feel for them, my heart goes out to them, but the base part of me recoils. It's as if this awfulness might be contagious. I feel I can't get too close, it's too raw. When we return the next morning, the bed has a different occupant.

•

IT'S REALLY HARD to see Edwyn put under again so soon after waking up. We've reassured him as best we could, never sure how much, if anything, he's taking on board, and then he's being wheeled off, with his various bits of technology stacked around him on the bed.

Myra, Petra and I go to the Starbucks round the corner and, when our restlessness gets the better of us, we go for a chilly walk on Hampstead Heath. It's been a freezing week since our troubles began. It's even snowed a few times. But mainly it's been that damp, bitterly cold weather that February specialises in; a miserable backdrop for all the to-ing and fro-ing to the hospital. The walk actually helps us relax a little and soon the time passes and Edwyn's back on the ward, with his new orifice, looking much more comfortable. The significance of a tracheostomy tube, the journey to be weaned off it, will soon unfold. What a voyage of discovery we are on.

Once his 'trachy' tube is in, Edwyn gets another type of tube, one that will become the bane of his life, a tremendous nuisance to his nursing staff and will drive me to the brink of a nervous breakdown. This is the blessed nasogastric tube, which goes up the nose, down the gullet and into the stomach. It's to deliver much needed nutrition and medication. His new nurse, Eleanor, as she hooks up the first bag of liquid food, turns to us with a grin and says, 'That's his steak and chips.' During the night Edwyn yanks the tube out for the first time. It is put back down again. A pattern is about to be established. A painful one.

•

EDWYN TAKES IT easy over the next couple of days. He gets slightly stronger, slightly more awake each day. He still only manages a few minutes with his eyes open before slipping back again into oblivion. He can't communicate, he tries to smile if you josh with him, he'll squeeze your hand if you squeeze his, but he has a very far-away look and I have no clue as to what his experience of all this strangeness is. He seems to be in no pain. Only irritated by the tube in his nose, which gets pulled out several more times. Constant vigilance is required.

•

TRYING TO GET everyone to eat is a struggle, and back at the homestead, tense competition is emerging. David's name for it – The Soup Wars. For those who are at home on relief from hospital duty there are hours to fill so, suddenly, everyone is making soup. David, Mum, Hazel, and Amete, my friend who has worked with me at home and in the studio for ten years. It will become a competitive business, this soup making. David reckons he is triumphant. My poor mum, Sadie, looks dubiously at the lentil soup she has made. Scottish women of her generation are generally past masters at homemade soup. They have tried and tested variations-on-a-theme down the generations, producing cast-iron, guaranteed winners. But she could only find Edwyn's fancy puy lentils in the cupboard and the resultant sludgy colour is worrying her. We reassure her it tastes great. I sample a bit of them all. I hate to admit it, but David rightly claims the crown. In a tight contest, he demonstrates exceptional natural ability. As our father used to say, 'The only thing holding me back is my modesty.'

•

ON THURSDAY MORNING I drive Will to school. Keen to go back, he is continuing with his normality formula. I give him a hug and watch with relief as his mate catches up with him and places a kindly hand on his shoulder. I look at them walk through the gate together and think about how brilliant teenage boys are.

•

A MERE SIX days after Edwyn arrived in ICU, Sean announces that he is to be moved to an neurosurgery unit on the tenth floor. There he will still receive intensive nursing, comparatively, but it's not the ICU idea of intensive and I feel panicky. Sean reassures me that this is the normal reaction. 'It feels so safe here, I know, but there is no way we would be moving him out if he needed to be here, I promise. He's a success story for us. We've been losing a lot of people recently. He's done brilliantly.' Then he leans over Edwyn and says, 'We can't keep you here any longer, mate, you're doing too well. I know you probably think that's mad, cos you feel like shit, but honestly it's true. We'll miss you, Edwyn.' Edwyn smiles wanly at him. What a pro.

But Edwyn is certainly not so safe away from this place. And from here on in, I'm back on duty, to keep my eyes and ears open for the inevitable failings and omissions. You may think this is evidence of my neurosis, my over-protectiveness, my anxiety. I have all these failings, admittedly, but hospital life gave me good reason. I would have to watch the staff like a hawk if Edwyn wasn't to experience unnecessary setbacks. I couldn't assume they had it under control. On some wards they did, sometimes, on some shifts, but it was scarily inconsistent care. I believe our hospitals do the critical, cutting-edge stuff quite brilliantly but the long-term therapeutic stuff, the less glamorous, coalface activity, well, inconsistent is a kind way to describe it. And when you're in the middle of it, you don't feel so kindly. I would swing from murderous to despairing. These were joys in store.

Edwyn remained in the neurosurgery unit for another five days, two of which included the weekend. Hospitals grind to a halt at the weekend. The tumult of the weekdays, when you can't get in the lifts or find a seat in the cafeteria, evaporates and time hangs heavy. Tumbleweed rolls along the corridors. There are hardly any doctors around. If you needed one you would be seen by someone extremely lowly, an overworked soul who covers the basics and only troubles his boss in an emergency, which you are convinced they would be unable to spot in any case. Edwyn would often be visited by a doctor of no fixed specialty, hedging his or her bets and avoiding making any decisions one way or the other, which was probably just as well.

Edwyn's care from this point forwards, although still involving high maintenance as he remained on breathing support and tube feeding, would be a matter of dogged routine. He would be seen regularly, at least once a day, by the team of super nurses from the critical care outreach team, one of whom was Richard, from Edwyn's first morning, and another, Jo, the nurse with dark hair and glasses who fought for his life on the ward that Friday morning. Until his tracheostomy comes out, he is still their patient. Over the coming weeks I will see Edwyn visibly brighten when either of these two appear at his bedside. From early on during his recovery he had an unerring instinct for who the good guys were, which was an immense source of relief to me. More evidence that his marbles were intact; he was still a great judge of character.

LIFE FOR US, his family, had become a succession of days, each a separate and distinct slice of endurance. For me, the time spent in hospital goes fast. I'm so absorbed by the detail of each procedure, each reading, each snippet of information. I watch everything that's going on, monitor every change, with my semi-deranged beady eye.

On admission to the neurosurgery ward I notice that Edwyn's tummy is distended. This is probably because he's having trouble processing the liquid food. His system has slowed right down. As the months pass I discover how obsessed hospital staff are with bowel regularity. Rightly so. An obstruction in a patient like Edwyn, immobilised, drugged, on breathing support, post-operative, is a real risk, with the worst case scenario involving surgery. But when I draw attention to the swelling a nurse asks me, 'Hasn't he naturally got a pot belly?'

So of course I scream back at her: 'Are you mental? Can't you tell the difference? What are you doing in this job? Have you any clue what this man has just been through?'

No, of course I don't. I don't say any of this out loud. I simply reply in the negative, quietly, while listening to the strange, high-pitched noise in my head and feeling my stomach muscles twist and turn just a little more.

Then Edwyn's blood pressure shoots up again. Will he go back to intensive care? I wish he would. I'm distracted with worry, beside myself.

This moment passes, gets dealt with, eventually, and we move on. And this is how it is, day by day. One small drama after another. One frustrating exchange following another.

•

TO PREVENT EDWYN from pulling his nasogastric tube out again, the nurses have placed a large, soft boxing glove on his wayward left hand. This is controversial. Some NHS staff believe it to be an abuse of human rights. Others see it as a necessary evil. I can see both sides of this argument. Of course, he hates it. He spends the afternoon trying to bite it loose. On Saturday night, my birthday, someone gives me permission to remove it for a while as long as I keep close watch. Edwyn is so relieved he takes my hand. Normally, we are not big on hand holding. Edwyn is touchy-feely phobic and I'm not far behind. When presented with other people indulging in public displays of affection, he would usually mutter, 'Doomed!'

Then he strokes my face. Dear God. We sit in the gloom like this for an hour.

•

SUNDAY 6 MARCH, two weeks to the day since Edwyn's admission, is another day of blood pressure worry. It keeps spiking up to the old scary levels. There is an experiment going on to find the correct daily balance of three types of medication. Edwyn's room is filled with the sound of the breathing machine and the beep of the pulse monitor. My

82

heart is in my mouth all day. And I have to say goodbye to Nan and Petra. They have jobs and children and other patients who need them.

At one point I'm sitting in the corridor outside Edwyn's room and I'm feeling just awful. The blood pressure worry is ongoing. From nowhere a smiling young male nurse approaches.

'Are you a mummy?'

'Yes...'

'Happy Mother's Day!' And he gives me a big hug. I hadn't noticed it was Mother's Day. And I'm laughing and crying. The kindness of strangers. What a lovely boy.

•

ON MONDAY, Myra and I arrive on the ward and are greeted by a sight both exhilarating and alarming. Edwyn is swinging above his bed in an electrically operated hoist, a giant sling-like thing. Richard from the ICU team is supervising as they lower him into a super beefed-up wheelchair, with support sections for every part of the body. He is completely limp, looks nothing like himself. Yet I'm very excited to see this giant leap, as well as a little horrified at his appearance.

Edwyn, we quickly realise, absolutely hates the experience of being upright. We know this because, miraculously, the staff have put the speaking valve into his tube. When asked questions, he weakly answers 'yes' or 'no'. So my joy at hearing his voice swiftly turns into a paroxysm of anxiety as he manages by exhausted gesture and sound to let us know how knackered he feels, how desperate to get horizontal, almost from the first moment he lands in the chair. It has to be done, but it's not easy to watch, this first thirty minutes out of bed. Later, when he can get his feelings out more effectively, he will refuse to be seated upright for that long. The sensations of nausea and vertigo, combined with his double vision, make it unbearable. For Edwyn, that thirty minutes must have seemed like eternity. It took a little while for the penny to drop for me; Myra got the message quicker that day. You live and learn.

•

A COUPLE OF days later, Edwyn is signed off by the neurosurgeons, whom I haven't seen again since those early days in intensive care (they do their rounds early in the morning, before I'm allowed in). We're suddenly on the move again. I had been told he would stay on the neurosurgery unit for a long time. Indeed the sister seems a little annoyed that he is being moved. It seems the stroke unit consultant has claimed him back as his patient.

It's incredible how little most doctors communicate with their patients and their families. Unbelievably, in 2005, it was still deemed entirely acceptable to keep relatives in the dark. Over Edwyn's time in hospital I had plenty of opportunity to analyse doctors in general. My theory is the obvious one. They are insecure, as competitive types usually are. Many are socially awkward. There are lots of cultural norms within the profession that they use to cover up their difficulties; aloofness, imperiousness, brusqueness. Many seem to absolutely loathe contact with relatives, particularly the most senior doctors. I didn't feel so much patronised as brushed aside, their discomfort palpable. They hate the internet, with its ready information and answers for the amateur. You have to screw up all your courage to persist with your questions, to face them down.

In the end though, I was not much bothered by this lack of good bedside manner, particularly from the neuro-surgeons. Given what they had done for Edwyn, the mind-boggling genius of it, I had nothing but gratitude and respect for them. I ventured once to thank the head of Edwyn's surgical team when we met again further down Edwyn's treatment road: 'I have no words to express how we feel. For everything you and your team have done for Edwyn, for all of us.'

'Well, you know what we always say,' he came back, unaccustomedly jaunty. 'Neurosurgeons one, God nil.'

My sister, the nurse, was apoplectic when I related this to her. The air was peppered with unrepeatable expletives. I didn't take such exception, rather delighting in the swag-ger of it.

•

OUR MOVE BACK to the stroke unit sees Edwyn positioned in a four-bed bay directly in front of the nurses' station. High dependency, they call this. The unit's manager, Pauline, who was on holiday when we were here before,

85

but has heard all about him, gives us a warm welcome. Edwyn's bay mates are Phyllis, Ronnie and Doris. Edwyn is the youngest person in this unit by quite some way and, although the place completely freaks poor Will out, viewing it as Hell's antechamber (to the extent that it I practically have to drag him in to see his dad twice a week, a position Edwyn has complete sympathy with for the duration of his stay), I feel Edwyn will be safer here. On this ward the staff work brutally hard. The nursing is largely unglamorous, nitty gritty, not to say mucky, stuff. And they really put their backs into it. These are the most dedicated nurses we will encounter, for this is not a fashionable, high-tech specialty. The unit crosses over with geriatrics (or God's waiting room, as some were wont to call it), the real Cinderella of the health service. It is a testing ground of nursing skill and dedication. All hospitals should be judged by the standard of care they mete out to these, the most vulnerable, and often least supported, souls in our midst. Many of them received only a few visitors and were pretty much without advocacy. They relied on Pauline (who led from the front), and her team, for human warmth at the tail end of their lives. Edwyn and I settled in for what would turn out to be five long weeks in the company of our newly discovered community of the vulnerable.

•

A YOUNG IRISH doctor talked to Edwyn and me many months later, in the canteen of a different hospital, about the squeamishness of the modern world when confronted with the realities of illness and death. Having travelled and worked in many parts of the world where strife, poverty and health problems walk together, and where people seemed to accept the bad stuff much more readily as part of the fabric, the balance even, of life, he reckoned we in the West have conspired to hide away from unpleasantness, to hermetically seal it off from our perception of normal life. Of course, this can't be done for ever, because most of us will have to deal with crises in our lives at some point. It can't be denied, this messy and unpleasant aspect of the human condition. There will be trauma and losses. But when they do occur, we are particularly ill-prepared in the modern world. I certainly felt this applied to me. During all the months Edwyn was in hospital and for many more afterwards, I wrestled with a sense of unreality and, sometimes, injustice. A longing for a return to our charmed life.

At times, in the strange moments between sleep and wakefulness, I almost believed I could will what was going on away. I would wake to the same feeling of intense anxiety again and again. I knew there was something vital I had omitted to do. A second ago, when I was asleep, I knew what it was. Now it was gone. I'd rack my brains to remember it. It was very real, this urgent sense of something needing to be attended to. But it would never come back. Soon, I could rationalise that it was a symptom of the situation; there wasn't anything urgent I'd missed. But I never quite believed that. The nagging sense that I was allowing something to slip through the cracks persisted, every morning, for most of the first year.

•

AROUND US, life really did go on. Casual, merciless, normal life was carrying on as usual as spring was bursting out all over lovely, leafy Hampstead, just outside the hospital doors. I resented it. Happy, healthy people strolling with their children in the sunshine, sitting in restaurants and cafes chatting, reading newspapers, shopping, laughing. And for a little while, I truly hated them for it. Horrible, but I couldn't help it.

But it seemed to me that Edwyn had joined a secret society of the sick, especially the long-term, really sick. Sometimes late at night I'd go to the cafeteria for a coffee or, in later weeks when he was eating and drinking again, to pick up cold bottles of water (I had to buy it in small bottles regularly because there was no way to prevent it from going lukewarm in the fetid heat of unventilated hospital wards, and there were no fridges to keep things cool. Do I sound moany?). Often there would be a huddled group somewhere, with the tight shoulders, the strained look around the eyes, the hushed and anxious tones, and I would know that tonight it was someone else's turn to take their place alongside us for a season in hell.

But here's the thing. I came to understand the inherent normality of what was happening to us. It's far from unique. Looking about me as I moved around the building, I knew our story was being replicated in different forms, some much, much worse, around the hospital, around the city, around the world, by *millions* of families. We were nothing special. Weeks later, while we were still in the Royal Free, Edwyn found his flow one day and said to me: 'Suffering is ordinary. Suffering is the understanding.'

He knew, too.

UNDERSTANDING

As THE DAYS rolled on, I began to take stock. The shocks kept coming as I found out the extent of Edwyn's injury. He was such a blessed boy, with so many gifts at his ready disposal from his early boyhood. An embarrassment of riches. He wore his abilities lightly, enjoyed and added to them as his life rolled out. And now life had come to an abrupt full stop and everything, virtually everything had to be tackled from scratch. The bleed in Edwyn's brain, like a heat-seeking missile, was bound and determined to destroy all the accomplishments of forty-five years. Facing up to the emerging evidence of all that was lost, the deficits, as they are known in the neurology trade, was nearly unbearable. I felt lost, engulfed by my terror, which was a constant, physical feeling in my throat.

The stroke, as I learned, was located in the left side of Edwyn's brain, in the frontal and parietal lobes. The damage was, as we had been told, extensive. What did this mean to Edwyn?

First of all it meant the loss of effective communication to his right-hand side, called haemaplegia. So he couldn't walk. Indeed, he couldn't roll onto his side, sit up, get out of bed unaided, stand. Edwyn was completely dependant for all physical functions. He was truly vulnerable, totally reliant on others for every aspect of his personal care. Marooned, he was one of the few fortunate recipients of an electrically operated bed with a three-way control, complete with air mattress to prevent pressure sores developing in the immobile patient. I had to be extra watchful when Edwyn was moved from ward to ward to ensure that the bed came with us. Such luxuries are at a premium in the NHS. Edwyn could be buzzed up to a sitting position, or semi-reclining, and his legs could be raised and lowered. But, unable to support himself, he would frequently slide down the bed in a slump. I was taught the technique for hauling him up to a more comfortable position and would execute this manoeuvre a couple of dozen times a day. To see your life partner, a moment ago an enormously able human being, reduced to such a condition is very hard to bear. Physically, he needed mothering, like a newborn baby. I found I was able to be practical in my response. There was no room for existentialist angst as Edwyn needed my help.

The stroke had disrupted Edwyn's speech and language function profoundly: he had aphasia. I had never heard of it, an admission that strikes me now as ludicrous, given how common it is. It's an umbrella term for the loss of speech, word finding, language comprehension, reading and writing, as a result of brain injury, most commonly, through stroke. A small and struggling organisation, called Connect, based in London, are the best and most vociferous advocates in this country of better understanding of the nature of aphasia. Unless a stroke or traumatic brain injury occurs in your family, it's likely that you will remain as much in ignorance of the condition as I did.

To begin with, his aphasia meant that he was virtually unable to speak at all. Indeed, although the *essence* of Edwyn still seemed strong, his thinking ability had clearly been blasted. He understood some of the things we said to him, or appeared to, but it was difficult to determine to what extent, as the ability to communicate linguistically had deserted him. Stupidly, I hadn't considered how this would impinge on reading and writing. The discovery that both these functions, taken for granted by almost all of us, and a huge part of Edwyn's life, were also gone, was profoundly shocking to me.

•

ACCORDING TO BRAIN science the left side of the brain is where speech and language are located. Also according to science, brain cells, once destroyed, are gone for good. Since Edwyn's stroke I have formulated a few amateur theories of my own, based on nothing more than observation. There used to be a fashionable quasi-medical craze that went around in late Victorian times called phrenology. You still see the china heads in antique shops, with the head mapped out in different regions for different character traits. I have come to think of some of the pronouncements made by doctors and research scientists into the workings of the human brain as a little too close to phrenology to take seriously.

The problem is largely centred on the egotism of science and the pecking order of those given the most credence. Neurologists would probably put themselves at the top of the pile. But no consultant or professor will spend the time that a speech and language therapist does with their patients. There are a great many eminent neurologists, aphasiologists, professors of neurolinguistics and neuropsychologists, and I would hazard that they all believe themselves to be superior academically to the humble speech and language therapist. But to my mind they can simply never hope to understand the reality of aphasia – how it attaches to the human experience – the way that specialist speech and language therapists, who assign hours each day to be with real live patients, do.

Over the last four years Edwyn has spent hundreds of hours with his therapists, Trudi Jenkins and Sally Ghibaldan. They are specifically experts in the field of speech and language impairment in adults with acquired brain injury. They are dedicated professionals, tailoring all their knowledge and experience to Edwyn's individual and ever-changing needs. They arrive prepared, they plan the way forward, but are never afraid to change tack if an approach isn't working. They learn from Edwyn and their other patients, and are continuously adding to the sum of their professional knowledge. But there is more to this dynamic duo than any of these words can convey. They are creative geniuses, fascinated and humbled by the unknowable nature of the brain and the spirit of its possessors. This really is the key thing. It's impossible to predict the path recovery will take. There are as many routes as there are human faces. This profession is certainly not given enough credit. The best therapists turn around lives that appear to be wrecked. From the first day Edwyn met Trudi, in a crowded and noisy hospital ward, five weeks into his illness, when he was adrift on a sea of chaos and loss, he put his trust in her utterly and lived for his sessions. For Edwyn, speech and language therapy in the hands of these two women has given him back meaningful life. Simple as that.

Whilst it's obvious that the majority of language exists *à gauche*, on the left, as Broca, an early French pioneer of brain mapping declared, there is more to this than meets the eye. As Edwyn has fought his way back to dealing with language, he seems to have defied the commonly held idea that brain cells do not regenerate. His knowledge of language had not been wiped out, although it may have first appeared to be so. Recovery has been a process of relocation, rediscovery, rewiring. As a witness to this process, I have watched an unfathomably complex work of reconstruction. Order from chaos. But then he was, in his old life, perfectly used to finding whatever he needed in the midst of chaos. He could recall the placement of every little piece of precious junk and ephemera and couldn't bear it if I or anyone else attempted to tidy it up. Maybe this ability hadn't deserted him as he ploughed through the miasma of confusing thoughts to locate his touchstones, his markers of familiar things that would lead him back to his store of knowledge. I have read reams of academic research material on Edwyn's condition. My view, albeit ill-informed and anecdotal, is that the science, although worthy in its intent, doesn't begin to scratch the surface of understanding. Sir Jonathan Miller, he of *Beyond the Fringe* fame amongst many other things, including a training in neurology, summarised it neatly when he said, 'Compared to the human brain, the universe is a clockwork toy.'

•

ON HIS FIRST night back on the stroke unit Edwyn is reunited with Sarah, his night nurse from a couple of weeks ago. Sarah is a grandmother, a big lady, whose size belies the way she zooms around the ward getting twice the amount of work done as youngsters half her age. She's shaking her head in disbelief that he's still here, but I'm delighted to see her. I know her and how good she is and I can leave him in her care with a happy heart.

Apart from our now familiar struggle with him yanking his feeding tube out, Edwyn settles in comfortably. In a way, being in the high dependency bay provides more visual entertainment, as we watch the busy ward day unfolding before us. Ronnie, beside Edwyn, has had a very deep stroke and is also on a trachy breathing tube. And this is where you start to see the upside, for Edwyn is doing a lot better than this soul. Ronnie has no means of communication, has a very bad chest which makes the most miserable noise. When you are on breathing support and have a tracheostomy, it's impossible to clear your lungs of their natural secretions and you have to have them hoovered out regularly with a disposable tube which is pushed down the trachy line. Suctioning, it's called. Apart from when he was on ICU, I had to alert staff to Edwyn's need to be suctioned each time I would hear him start to rattle. It's not a good idea to let that stuff accumulate. It thickens and hardens and then is a bloody nightmare to loosen. And that is how you get pneumonia. I saw this happen to Ronnie. I wasn't going to let it happen to Edwyn if I could help it. I heard many months later that Ronnie did eventually get off the trachy, to the credit of the nursing team on Berry Ward. But at this time Edwyn appeared to making galloping progress compared to Ronnie.

Opposite, Doris is very ill and heavily sedated. Her husband Jack is with her all day. He's eighty-five and has the energy of an athlete. He proudly shows me a picture of Doris when she was a young mother with their sons. It's in one of those old-fashioned keyrings where you press a button and a light comes on behind a tiny photo, which you view through a magnifying spy hole. I haven't seen one of these since I was a kid. The photo was taken at a holiday camp in the 60s. Doris is done up to the nines, with bright blue eye shadow and orange lipstick.

'Isn't she gorgeous? Five sisters and I got the best of the bunch,' Jack tells me.

David and Jack strike up a friendship. He's a proper cockney geezer, with stories about his wartime experiences as a Desert Rat with Monty. Talking about Rommel and the Afrika Korps he says, 'I'll tell you what, they were brilliant soldiers. Much better than us. I haven't a clue how we managed to beat them, tell you the truth!'

He heads home every night to make his tea, and he always tells Edwyn and me what he's having: 'I got a nice bit of liver and onions ...'

In the midst of his own sorrows, he cheers Edwyn on, telling him how he's young, he'll beat this.

During the quietness of the first Saturday afternoon in the unit, I'm looking at Edwyn when a slow smile spreads across his face. I get positive proof that, stroke or no, his hearing is still miles better than mine, when he points across at Jack, who is sitting beside Doris, his face close to hers, and singing very softly.

Before she died they moved Doris into a single room and we didn't get to say goodbye to Jack.

•

ANOTHER MILESTONE FOR me comes when Edwyn has the speaking tube in and says to me, in his tiny, whispery voice: 'Be careful with William.'

He repeats it, with difficulty, several times.

His first sentence, and one I imbue with enormous significance. Looking back, I'm not sure he was really able to control these little surprise pronouncements, but on that day, it was pure gold. I, of course, assumed that he was expressing his deep concern that the impact of the powerful and frightening events of recent times would take its toll eventually on our son. How can it be coincidence that this was the first sentence he uttered?

•

THAT FIRST WEEKEND back on the unit it feels as though we finally cross the Rubicon in terms of the evil nasogastric tube. Edwyn pulls it out for about the millionth time. OK, maybe the nineteenth time. And just for good measure he pulls the trachy tube out too. This goes back in relatively easily but his throat has had enough and the feeding tube won't go back in. This is horrible. Various people have several goes, each to no avail. Richard appears and asks Edwyn if he can bear to put up with him having another attempt. Edwyn submits himself to the torture one more time. As Richard leans over to begin, Edwyn lets rip a mighty fart.

'More tea, vicar?' says Richard, deadpan.

But even he is unsuccessful. Oh, hell.

They decide it will have to be inserted using an endoscope, a camera to guide it down. This happens in a special suite downstairs, for which you need to be allocated a slot.

We wait all afternoon. Edwyn's had no drug treatments, no nutrition bags, he's dehydrating and I'm losing it. At one point a dolt of a junior doctor tries to explain that the endoscopy suite is very busy with various emergency patients that need to be seen before they shut down for the weekend. Edwyn's at the end of the queue. And if time runs out? What then? No food, no drugs, no water until Monday? Well, that can't happen. So then he'll become an emergency and something might finally be done.

Now, you may think that I'm exaggerating but this was my repeated observation. Hospitals operate on a crisis management policy, not crisis prevention. Don't anticipate the bad thing that's round the corner and do whatever it takes to avoid it; just wait for it to happen and then figure out what to do. It's just nuts. I had to find the junior doctor's superior, haul him round the corner out of earshot of Edwyn, and threaten, in a controlled hiss, to go up like a rocket in a way that would completely spoil his boss's weekend. He got on the phone and, an hour and a half later, in the nick of time, the endoscopy happened. Even so, what should have taken five minutes took forty. I paced the corridor outside the suite in a cold sweat, not knowing what was happening in there, imagining Edwyn's pain as they struggled to get the thing in place again. That night, I ask for the boxing glove. I tape it up in ten different ways to make it Edwyn-proof. I have never seen him look at me with such pure venom as I kiss him goodnight. He turns away from me in disgust.

Outside the ward, I fall into Hazel's arms in abject misery. We head for the station to pick up David and the two of them console me.

Early next morning I call to ask how Edwyn is. 'Very cheerful,' Pauline informs me. 'He and Janet (another night nurse) seem to have reached an understanding during the night. The glove is off.'

Oh no.

'The tube's still in. I don't know what she said but it seems to have done the trick.'

I don't know to this day what she said, something about defending his right to suffer pain I think, but he didn't pull it out again … for another week.

•

DAVID IS WITH us for the weekend and stays until Monday lunchtime, so he can come with me for moral support to a family meeting with the consultant and the ward team. This doctor, a general physician, sees Edwyn only for a few minutes every couple of days on his ward round, but considers himself qualified to predict his long-term prospects, even at this very early stage. He is followed wherever he goes by a retinue of medical students, which he assembles, standing in a respectful semicircle behind his chair. After asking ward sister Pauline to silence a noisy elderly man outside on the ward ('Somebody shut that up, please!'), he proceeds to inform us that Edwyn is in a very bad way, with little chance of meaningful recovery.

Apparently, the progress a patient makes in the first three weeks is a good indication of their long-term outcome. This, regardless of the fact that Edwyn's been recovering from brain surgery, coma, etc. He tells us that within the next six months or so, we should expect to be glad to see Edwyn able to sit up unaided and perhaps able to make an assisted transfer from bed to a wheelchair. And any progress we may see could plateau and finish at any time. As for his speech, his cognitive powers, well, not much going on there, I'm afraid.

David and I pass silent judgement on this charmer.

I really want to talk about Edwyn's next move, on to neuro-rehabilitation. It proves very difficult to get a straight answer from Dr Insensitive on this subject but I eventually pin him down at the end of the meeting.

This is the verdict: the availability of beds in specialist rehab units is very limited and the waiting lists are lengthy. Entry to these units is by assessment. The patient needs to demonstrate potential for recovery. These places are very results driven, I will discover. The point of their existence is to be able to present a demonstrable before and after picture. During Edwyn's time in hospital, one way they aimed to achieve this was by excluding anyone over sixty, a practice since outlawed as it transgresses several European laws. Strangely, the moral repugnancy of such selection criteria didn't seem to occur to anyone.

I ask, then ask again in a more insistent way, because the response is woolly, if Edwyn can be placed on these lists immediately. Inwardly I resolve to press on with my own research. It's already clear that I'll have to make a nuisance of myself to get things moving. That's fine, I have no problem with that. I say, flatly, 'Thank you for your candour,' (which impresses David), and we bring the meeting to a rather abrupt end.

We step out of the office and across the ward I see Edwyn. He looks so lost, so fragile, and my heart swells. I will fight for him, I will protect him. He's at the mercy of bastards like this for the time being, but they won't have the final say on his destiny.

HOME LIFE

EDWYN'S HOSPITAL SOJOURN was stretching ahead of us in an endless succession of days. Some good days, some bad days. A pattern, of sorts, began to emerge.

I would wake after a fitful night, usually with the light still on because of my bad habit of reading myself to sleep, and wake Will up for school. Big teenager though he was, I regressed to babying him a bit at this time. He would transfer from the bath to the couch in the living room, where I would serve him his breakfast on a tray. I'd lay out his school gear and then we'd watch TV, usually an American sitcom called *Everybody Loves Raymond*, which started at eight o'clock. Will used to say the grandparents in it were totally his Granny and Grandaa. This was a nice bit of the day. Then I'd drive him to school. This wasn't always such a nice bit of the day. Getting out of the house in the morning, usually running late, is a flashpoint that many will recognise. On one of my ranting and raving mornings, I wailed at him, 'How many more of these car fights do you think I can take?'

'Oh yeah? Try being me, stuck with Shouty McShoutington of Shoutytown every fucking morning!'

You've got to give it to him.

Unless he came to visit his dad in hospital, which he did on average twice a week, because he absolutely hated it – not Dad, but hospital – this would be the last I would see of Will until about nine or ten o'clock at night. At first I would try to get him to come more often, but Edwyn was on Will's side, entirely understanding, so I stopped the nagging.

I would return from school to tackle the minutiae of daily life which stubbornly persists, heedless of surrounding drama. Put a wash load on, tidy up, make phone calls, send emails, pay bills. Then assemble my kit bag for the day and set off for the hospital, usually arriving around eleven.

Running the gauntlet past the bedraggled band of smokers who congregated at the hospital entrance, freezing in their hospital gowns and pyjamas, a few of them amputees, all of them with hacking coughs ('Morning, everyone ...' – we were all familiar faces to each other), sometimes handing over a couple of quid to the regular panhandlers who, very astutely, have worked out that around a hospital there will be lots of people who would not dare tempt Fate by refusing a request for dosh. I certainly wouldn't. Down the corridors of the ground floor reception area, experiencing as I went the daily delight that was the Royal Free art exhibition. So much bad art in such a small space. The longer I looked at it the more extraordinarily bad it seemed. The packed-like-sardines lifts, where everybody ignores each other, in spite of, or perhaps because of, our close proximity. And then through the doors of the ward, breathing through my mouth in advance to avoid the horrible smell of Jeyes fluid which hits you as you push through the swing doors. I always felt an uneasy mixture of anxiety and guilt as I drew near to Edwyn. After all, I'd escaped from the place overnight, for hours. He was stuck fast in bed, powerless to direct his own existence. He would always be so relieved to see me, which would swell the guilty feeling.

I'd begin my routine, tidying and setting up everything we needed for our day: clean clothes in, dirty ones out. Give him a shave if he needed it. Maybe a manicure or pedicure. By the time I arrived in the morning the nurses on the stroke ward would have bedbathed him. Try to tidy his hair, about which he used to be so obsessive.

When we first lived together, Edwyn's hair was a major bone of contention. He had a high-maintenance quiff, which took a very long time to assemble. How I grew to loathe it, this symbol of vanity. Often, it would go wrong, and he would start again from scratch. The main component of the operation was Extra Hard Hold Elnett hairspray. Choking clouds of the stuff. We were late for *everything* because of the quiff. I would be showered, dressed and made up in twenty minutes. I would stomp around the flat, screaming my frustration. But no, if the quiff wasn't up to scratch, we were going nowhere. Looking at pictures of him recently, I was reflecting on his handsomeness and wondering why I didn't appreciate it more at the time. Edwyn was looking at them too. 'Ah, I miss my quiff.'

Of course, that was it. The enemy. I had almost forgotten. 'I bloody don't...'

I was almost rid of the thing once, around 1988. Edwyn was sitting on the kitchen floor, by the big full-length mirror, his hairdressing station, doing the quiff in readiness for a show at the National Ballroom in London that evening. Steve Skinner, guitar player and, luckily for Edwyn, possessor of a strong sense of smell, leapt up suddenly, shouting: 'What's that smell?'

He bounded towards Edwyn, grabbed the can of mousse from his hands and yelled: 'It's fooking hair remover, you nutter!' (He's from Bridlington.) Mine, of course. Edwyn had mistaken it for a hair product.

Panic stations. We got him into the bathroom and under the shower head in the nick of time. This stuff works fast – he was minutes from instant baldness. He has never looked so terrified. I have seldom laughed so much.

Towards the end of the 90s, in his late thirties, a female TV interviewer was lamenting the quiff's disappearance.

'Well, unfortunately, I'm beginning to get a bit thin on top and the quiff was starting to resemble the conductor on *On The Buses*. So it was time for it to go.'

Right now, post-operatively, Edwyn's hair looked mad.

One side completely shaved off, the other far too long, like Bobby Charlton in a stiff breeze. I almost asked a visiting hairdresser to have a go, but was stopped by Greg, one of the charge nurses. I used to refer to this young man as Greg, the New Wave Nurse, because he looked like a trendy indie music fan, a bit like Jarvis Cocker. It turned out he did know loads about music, including Edwyn, and didn't reckon Edwyn would approve of the job this woman would make. Truthfully, the state it was in, anything would have been an improvement. Still, Greg's aim was true. He knew what men like himself and Edwyn felt about their hair. Super fusspots.

•

I HAD A selection of flasks for hot and cold things, one with ice with which to chill Edwyn's water or for ice therapy, the highly technical term for icing a spoon to help stimulate sensation on the right-hand side of his face and inside of his mouth, to encourage tidy feeding.

I would bring a selection of books for us to look at. An unexpected bonus was finding William's birth certificate in the back of one of them: a beautiful handwritten form in fountain pen from the Glasgow registry office, near where he was born. I had been missing it for ages and was hopping up and down with glee in the ward when it turned up inexplicably in the back of *Collins Book of British Birds*. I had brought in the book to try his memory of one his life-long passions: birds, especially British ones, on which subject he was an expert.

I would read the newspaper to Edwyn, trying him on the headlines. Pope John Paul II was very ill at this time, on the way out, in fact, and I'd keep Edwyn abreast of his progress: 'Guess what, the Pope has had a trachy op like you. I don't see him getting off it anytime soon. Unlike you.'

Then there were flash cards of animals and objects to stimulate his verbal memory. Writing and drawing materials. I found Will's fifteenth birthday cards the other day and we looked in amazement at Edwyn's impossible attempt at a signature, the 'Dad' a completely illegible scribble.

So the day would slip by. Strangely enough, time seemed to pass quite quickly for me. Edwyn's care was a constant thing. And I would talk to him lots and lots. I think he didn't mind; I hope so. We have always been pretty good gossips and I can yack for Scotland. So I would reminisce, fill him in on the latest about family, friends, Will's exploits. I would revisit past experience, recount old favourite stories, test his memory.

•

I WAS VERY excited to get a snatch of a chorus of a song from him one day. I was reminding Edwyn of when Alan, who ran Postcard Records, had his own band in the late 70s. They were called Oscar Wild. Without the 'e'. All the members had a punk name. Alan was Alan Wild. The guitar player was Brian Superstar. And the bass player was a girl called Janice Fuck. At the only gig they ever did, at Troon

Burgh Hall, Alan was resplendent in a Tom Jones-style, electric-blue frilly shirt. Janice had had some classical training in opera singing and Edwyn used to do an impression of their version of The Troggs song, 'I Can't Control Myself'. Alan would start, in his camp, lispy voice: 'I can't stand still cause you got me going . . .'

And then, apparently, according to the Edwyn story, Janice Fuck would echo in full soprano: 'Bah bah bah bah bah bah bah bah bah!'

You have to hear him do it for the full effect.

As I was delighting Edwyn with my own rendition of Oscar Wild in all their glory, he suddenly piped up, 'Whoa whoa whoa whoa, dustbin . . .'

Alan always claimed that this song was pure invention on Edwyn's part, that they never did any such thing. A typical Edwyn absurdist flight of fancy.

Apocryphal or not, I squealed in delight that he could remember something as daft as this. The important stuff was still intact.

•

WHEN EDWYN SLEPT, which he did often, I would slip out and buy his dinner, run errands, make calls. I became a regular, once a day, for a large glass of red wine in the Garden Gate, the pub down the road from the hospital. I loved that pub.

Sometimes Edwyn would have visitors. This was a slow trickle, as people were never sure when it would be appropriate to come and see him. Obviously this had not been possible for quite a few weeks; a long time for the fear of the unknown to take shape. Seb came first, and seeing him gave me a chance to reflect on how devastating the news of Edwyn's illness had been on those who were close to him, especially those who worked with him. And how scary it must have been to come and see him for the first time, with no real idea of what to expect.

Paul Cook, who as well as being a legendary Sex Pistol and fellow muso of Edwyn's, who had drummed with him on records and on tour since 1993, came to see him for the first time early on. A strong man, a proper grown up, he held it all together that day, which was a chaotic one. As he left us, Edwyn was lying in a corridor waiting to have a scan done. Something about Paul's retreating back as he walked away told me how hard it was for him to see his old friend in these circumstances.

•

AND SO ANOTHER day would draw to a close. I would help Edwyn to brush his teeth, have a bit of a wash, make sure his arm was in a comfortable position with a pillow underneath (with the haemaplegia, the arm was limp and heavy and a degree of subluxation – dislocation – had set in. Simply described, this means the arm, heavy with paralysis, falls out of the socket at the shoulder. If it's not supported in the correct position, it can become excruciatingly painful), see he had plenty of tissues and the nurse call button in a prominent place (even though I knew he couldn't use it), gather up all my stuff, kiss him goodnight and walk away, looking back at his abandoned form until I turned the corner.

Sometimes I'd take the train, but often, after I'd sussed out the local parking, I'd drive, mainly because I couldn't face the utter desolation of sitting in a deserted Hampstead rail station late at night. I preferred to give vent to the feelings that overwhelmed me at the end of the day in the privacy of the car, with Willie Nelson and Kris Kristofferson for company.

Arriving home and catching up a little with Will was always a relief, although extracting conversation from him was like drawing teeth. Best not to torture him. I would always get a hug, whether he liked it or not, before he went to bed. A teenage boy's thoughts can be off limits at the best of times and these times were certainly not that. I was wary of pushing too hard. We were just doing what we could to get through this thing. I'd look at my messages, do a bit of research, sink a glass of wine and head for bed and another night with my thoughts.

•

I HAD BUNKED off hospital early one night in late March to see Will's youth theatre workshop performance, *Totally Over You*. By this time the workshop leaders had heard from a couple of his mates what had happened to Will's dad and told me how amazed they had been at the unruffled front he had maintained. They dedicated the show to Edwyn, which I found terribly affecting. The play was so great, genuinely funny and full of attitude. Very funny theme song too, which they had properly recorded. I managed to work out the video camera (formerly Edwyn's department) sufficiently to get about ten minutes' worth to show Edwyn. I didn't quite master the battery charger (I know, it's tragic), so that was the lot.

But Will was definitely neglected for the duration of the hospital stay, with some pretty rotten consequences. It has just occurred to me that I have virtually no idea what he ate for most of these months. I would leave things in the fridge but he almost never had them. Hazel would try to get him to come to Islington for tea but he rarely did. Sometimes my mum would be there for a week or two to see what was going on, but the rest of the time he was pretty much left to his own devices, with an empty house to come home to. As the weather got better he would hang in the street a bit which led, perhaps unsurprisingly, to trouble.

On his own one evening, he got beaten up by several kids, one of whom he had known for a while, a kid called Sam. I knew him too, in fact he'd been in our house often when he was living nearby. He'd moved away but came back to hang out and I think doing Will over was partly to ingratiate himself with this lot. They'd tried to get Will to let them into the house which, of course, he wouldn't do. Coming home to discover what had happened, I made enquiries around the neighbourhood, but my efforts to find any of the boys were fruitless. A night or two later, however, when I had just got back from hospital, my doorbell rang. On the doorstep were several of Will's friends with Sam in tow. They had spotted him on Kilburn High Road and it seemed they'd kicked him all the way to my door, to force him to confront and apologise to Will. He was terrified. Rough justice. While appreciating that they were defending their friend in his hour of need, I had to nip the whole thing in the bud, before it got out of hand. I sent Sam on his way, advised him to lie low for a while and told Will's mates in the firmest terms that, whilst I loved them for their loyalty, this was where it ended.

By this time my mum had arrived for a visit and I was happy to think that William's outdoor wings would be clipped for a while.

To my horror, at the hospital next day I got a call from her. Sam had turned up at my door again, this time with his mother and a very aggressive older sister, who had shoved my mum aside in order to get at Will and wallop him. Somehow, at four foot eleven and aged seventy, my mum had managed to get this mentalist back over the doorstep and the door shut on them. The mother was screaming various threats through the door, so Mum suggested the police were called to deal with the matter, whereupon they scarpered. At home that night, we're trying to think about the best way to deal with all this nonsense, when the door bell goes again. This time it's Sam's dad, who is separated from the mum, but with whom

Sam actually lives, all the way from south London, with his son beside him. He is at least calmer, and when I speak to him, he immediately looks at his boy to confirm that what I have said is the truth. One look tells him that it is. He begins to regale me with his family difficulties. While sympathetic, the world is starting to take on that familiar surrealist tinge again and I have to emphasise that I cannot tolerate any more teenage rubbish as I have my own troubles. Off they go.

Meanwhile the effect upon my mum, the pensioner with attitude, appears to be that she's shed about forty years. I'm instantly transported back to a time when she could scare the knickers off all of us. You definitely do not want to mess with Sadie Keenan in a state of righteous indignation.

End of the story? Oh dear no. This crazy boy and his nasty mates come back a few weeks later and do Will all over again, right outside the front door. A local couple come to his rescue before too much physical damage is done, but he's frightened and furious. He looks like he's falling apart. This time we go straight to the police and file a report. Then the dad is back at the door when I'm not there. He leaves his number. I call him and he tells me Sam has been threatened again by Will's mates, around the corner from my house. I tell him about the latest attack and the police report and point out how easy it is for Sam and his family to find us when I have no idea where he lives, miles away, and that when his psycho son has a go at my boy I'm left helpless with impotent fury. He tells me his son should be entitled to walk wherever he likes and I agree. I invite him to come past my house the next day so that I can call the cops, tell them I've located the offender and leave the whole sorry mess to them. Will and I need this kid and his entire dysfunctional family right out of our lives for good, or so help me, I tell him. It finally ends.

SUCCESSES & SETBACKS

I'd ask for new directions
But my memory is short and full of holes
Still my recall's near perfection when compared with
the condition of my soul
The madness that surrounds me
The further that I roam
Directions that confound me
I can't find my way home...
~ Written in Stone, 2004

FOR MANY WEEKS music was a no-go area for Edwyn. One of the first things I brought him in hospital was his Walkman, but he firmly refused to listen to it. A little portable radio, also rejected. I'm not sure why. Was it too painful to listen to or was he unable to recognise or process it? I couldn't be sure, but it was worrying. He was adamant. No

music. At least none with any meaning to him. On a Saturday morning early on in our hospital life, a nurse placed a
radio tuned to Heart FM on the windowsill nearby. The
anodine middle-of-the-road strains left no impression on
Edwyn, as if he wasn't even hearing it. I would try again
further down the line, with happier results.

Edwyn had another major obstacle to using a radio or
a Walkman, though. Since the stroke he had severe dyspraxia.
If you have children of school age you may have heard this
term bandied around. It's part of the modern lexicon of
terms used in the craze for pathologising normal childhood
behaviour. It was suggested to me that perhaps William
had dyspraxia when he was at primary school. Also,
dyslexia, ADHD and even Asperger's Syndrome. Take your
pick. These random diagnoses came mainly from other
parents, anxious to find a label for any behaviour that was
less than perfect.

Edwyn's dyspraxia was a different animal. It meant that
he could not plan or sequence anything. A toothbrush was
confusing, as was a fork, to begin with. He would begin a
task, however small, and then freeze, completely blank as to
what to do next. I would combine verbal guidance with lots
of mime; I would demonstrate the move as I described it in
words. That helped a lot. It was months before he mastered
the control for his electric bed; simply up and down. A
remote control or a phone was out of the question, as was
the call button for a nurse. If the completed thought of
something he needed or wanted took place in his head, he

needed someone to be there to interpret it right away, or the thought would simply fly away. It seemed he couldn't make the link between wanting something, working out that he needed to ask a nurse for it, and that in order to do that he would have to call one, and in order to do that he would have to locate the button and press it. Even if he had managed this sequence, the chances of anyone understanding what he wanted were slim, so the whole exercise was somewhat doomed. This was one of the reasons why taking my leave of him at night filled me with such dread.

There's no accusation here. Nobody could be expected to read his mind and understand what he was getting at the way I did. I had all the time in the world and twenty years of life together to fall back on.

•

IN WEEKS THREE to five of hospital life, I was coming to grips with Edwyn's state of being. He couldn't move any part of his right-hand side, not even a toe wiggle. The first night he did just that I almost jumped out of my skin. I saw the sheet move above his right foot.

'Did you try that? Can you do that again?'

I was still doing all the talking at this time. He looked at me, raised an eyebrow and did it again. I called the nurse to witness that I wasn't losing it, that Edwyn could wiggle on demand. The beginning of movement.

But it would be a long time before Edwyn was anything less than fully dependent for every physical function. On the

stroke unit, there was a rudimentary amount of physiotherapy, delivered by a well-meaning but terribly patronising
team of physios. They spoke in that clichéd, slow-witted
style specially reserved by some people for conversations
with the elderly. And they seemed to be constantly reminding us of how incredibly busy and important they were, as
if to underline how fortunate we all were to receive a
modicum of their time and attention. I arrived one morning
a little late, to find Edwyn in the big supported wheelchair,
his back to me, facing the window, in a semi-slump. As I
approached, his stricken face came gradually more into view.
A mixture of panic, humiliation, frustration and fury. How
long had he been there? It seemed somewhere between one
and two hours. I held and reassured him, then manoeuvred
him back to bed. When he was settled and comfortable, I
gathered myself together and went in search of the fools
responsible.

The justification given was that the physios thought it
might be nice for him to look out at the world for a while.
So, I offered to reciprocate this lovely treat: 'How about I
strap you to a chair, completely immobilised, gag you, turn
you to face a grimed-up window so that you can't even
make eye contact with anyone and finally, walk off without
giving you any clue as to how long you'll be left there?
Fancy it? Can you imagine it?'

•

BY WEEK EIGHT Edwyn could draw his foot up along the bed.
His knee would collapse outwards, but never mind. By week

fifteen he would move on to drawing his foot up, keeping the knee steady for a while and lift his hip up from the bed a little. Slow progress, but no matter, progress all the same.

•

THE DREADED TUBE feeding was continuing. But the day was dawning when Edwyn's tracheostomy tube was coming out. He had made super-fast progress in his breathing which meant he was requiring fewer and fewer oxygen top-ups. And the important thing, his ability to clear his own lungs unaided (something we all do hundreds of times a day without realising it), was back to normal. Jo, his critical care outreach nurse, and definitely one of his favourite people on earth at this time, was very impressed with his healthy cough, which was so strong that he regularly fired the little cap out of the trachy tube, leaving me scrambling around the ward floor to find it. One embarrassing evening he managed a bullseye on a visitor.

On the red-letter day of complete removal, Edwyn yanked the feeding tube out of his nose again, but on this occasion, for the last ever time. The plan had been to replace the nasogastric tube with one going directly into the tummy but, fortunately, there was a long wait for this operation. Having tested that Edwyn was swallowing properly and not aspirating (breathing-in) liquids, the decision was made to give normal feeding and drinking a whirl. Provided we could keep his nutrition and hydration at the requisite levels, the plan for the tummy tube would be abandoned.

Pure, undiluted joy.

And I would be in charge. It would be my responsibility to fill in the chart, to select what he ate and drank. Well, nobody actually said this, I just sort of made the assumption. By this time my relationship with the majority of the ward staff was very relaxed. I wasn't that much of a pain and did my best to make myself useful. For instance, do you know how to change the sheets on a bed with an immobile six foot one man still in it? I do. I watched and learned. I am also now an expert shaver of a man's face (fortunately, those skills have now been retired indefinitely).

•

AT FIRST, we had to explore the parameters of soft food, high-calorie drinks and lots of water. Lots and lots of water. I badgered and plagued Edwyn with drinks of water. The stuff of life. It drove him nuts for months and years to come. I'm still at it to this day.

As I believe I have already mentioned, I'm no great shakes as a cook, but I do love shopping for food and fortunately we were spoilt for choice in the neighbourhood of the Royal Free. I fed Edwyn from delis and restaurants all over Hampstead, with some firm favourites quickly emerging. Thoughts of devising the perfect, nutritionally balanced, temptingly delicious diet consumed my waking hours. Edwyn has always been a fish and seafood fan, with meat not figuring hugely in his preferences. But at this time he was a full-blown carnivore, craving red meat like a maniac.

Minced beef figured heavily in the early days. Lasagnes, cottage pies, chillies, bolognese. He would have had this kind of food twice a day, very happily, and often did. Of course, it's a protein thing, and assisted the healing. His appetite was satisfyingly prodigious. It was such a great feeling to watch him eat himself stronger, a little more each day. Many ancillary staff members looked at me askance as we turned each hospital meal politely away. Did we think we were too good for it? But equally, many of them understood and nobody actually challenged my decision to refuse the stuff they served on the ward.

Where to start on the topic of hospital food? This is a distinctly depressing subject. And I'm no precious, fussy, North London foody. I was raised on the plain fare of industrial Lanarkshire in the 60s and 70s and will happily eat most things. But I do like food to be composed mainly of foodstuffs. British hospital food is extremely nasty stuff, which starts with the smell. That's when you know that it's full of unmentionable ingredients, masked with fake food aromas from the weird additives they use to conceal the true composition. The whole lot arrives, in some suspended animation form, ready to heat, on trucks from factories in South Wales. I have no idea how anyone can be expected to get better on this muck. And the flowery descriptions used on the hospital menus just add insult to injury.

Lucky Edwyn to be able to avoid it. But I wished I could have fed the whole ward. To see the older patients pushing their food around and off their plate, struggling with their impairments and the unedifying lumps in front of them. A really sad sight. It's a national disgrace. The majority of people in hospitals are, for obvious reasons, old, and obviously, many of them need quite a lot of assistance with eating and drinking. Low staff levels make it very difficult to get around every patient at every mealtime who needs help. I know, because I saw it; thousands of elderly people are lying in hospitals around the country – this sophisticated, enlightened land of ours – undernourished and dehydrated.

I had an idea. For the duration of their time in office, the health secretary, the prime minister and the cabinet should be fed the same food they serve up to patients. At all official government dinners and lunches. I've heard several of them wax lyrical about the healthy values of modern hospital menus and the progress being made, so it shouldn't be too much hardship. Tuck in, folks.

Edwyn's speech and language condition, as I mentioned earlier, is called aphasia. From a wordless beginning, the complexities of his problems were beginning to reveal themselves. But in so doing, I also witnessed improvement taking place, albeit almost imperceptibly. When you spend ten or so hours a day with someone, you notice every tiny development. From early on, with the speaking tube in, Edwyn would occasionally fire off a random statement. But it was impossible for him to harness language for general communication. Edwyn's speech had been assessed by the ward therapist, who then went on to inform me that he would receive no speech and language therapy on the stroke unit.

Their service was so badly funded that they were only able to cover swallowing problems. I accepted this without surprise and asked if I would be allowed to find my own therapist. She had no objection to this and neither had ward sister Pauline.

Trudi Jenkins came into our lives on Easter Sunday, 27 March 2005. I found her on the internet after calling several other therapists who I didn't get a good feeling about. What guided me to her, this woman who was destined to make such an incalculable impact on our lives? Accidental or meant to be, I'm forever grateful to have stumbled upon her. After a lengthy assessment she diagnosed Edwyn with severe expressive and less severe receptive aphasia. What on earth was this?

It is estimated that 250,000 people in Britain suffer from aphasia. Due to the symptoms of the condition, these people are unable to make a big noise, stand up for themselves. And when non-affected members of the public, or indeed the health service, encounter aphasia, they often mistake it for intellectual deficiency. Aphasia, or dysphasia as Edwyn prefers to call it, comes in myriad forms, but essentially it is a neurological interruption of the ability to locate, understand and express language.

The expressive side of language covers talking and writing. The receptive side is listening, understanding and reading. Edwyn was seriously affected in all areas, but most markedly in word finding, talking, reading and writing. He struggled to comprehend the meaning of what was being said to him, but by about three weeks into our stay on the stroke unit, I felt I could get there, and although the problems in this area were clear, I knew that with patience, they could be got around.

I held it as an article of faith that nothing had changed in Edwyn's underlying intellect, his perceptiveness, his instincts. I observed that thoughts were hard to pin down, but sometimes he displayed such insight and resourcefulness at getting his meaning across, even early on, that I always felt entirely positive that his latent ability to process the meaning of language was intact. It just had to be gently brought back into focus. And I had found the perfect person to help him do this in Trudi.

An example was on the day of Trudi's second or third appointment. The occupational therapist and a student arrived around two in the afternoon to fit Edwyn with a made-to-measure rigid plastic splint for his hand and wrist, to try and reduce tightness, or spasticity. I had earlier told Edwyn that Trudi would be coming at three, but wasn't sure if he understood the time, or numbers. Anyway, I'd written 3 pm down and showed it to him in addition to telling him in words. The splint business dragged on as the first attempt went wrong and Edwyn was getting increasingly agitated. He was trying so hard to tell me something and I had no clue as to what it was. I was doing my process of elimination routine, which wasn't foolproof because he often said 'no' when he meant 'yes' and vice versa, and we were getting nowhere fast. At last he pointed to the curtains which were pulled around him and gestured for me to pull them aside. Baffled, I did so. The curtains gone, the wall clock was revealed and he pointed to it insistently. The penny dropped.

'You're worried we won't be finished in time for Trudi's appointment?'

'Yes! Yes!' Edwyn's face crumpled with tears of pain and relief. I joined in with him, as the occupational therapists looked on awkwardly. But I was anxious to tell him how amazing it was that he worked out the time, remembered the appointment, and had found a way to get his anxiety across. His sessions with Trudi had become so important to him already. This little story summarises in one the agony of aphasia and the wonderful sense of power and triumph when you find a way to circumvent it.

Sitting silently alongside Edwyn and Trudi as they worked together was a revelation, a steep learning curve. I could never have understood the true nature of the aphasia without her. It was fascinating and horrifying at the same time.

At Trudi's first appointment, Edwyn was stuck on the first of many mantras that would develop along the way. Each time he tried to speak, the same thing would be produced. 'Grace Maxwell. Grace Maxwell. Grace Maxwell.'

Never Grace, always my full title. I would arrive in the morning and be greeted by, 'Oh, Grace Maxwell!'

Whereupon I would shake his hand and say, 'Correct, pleased to meet you, Edwyn Collins.'

I trace this back, rightly or wrongly, to years of mockery, since passed on to his son. When I answered the phone back in the old flat, I used to say my full name. I have a fairly strong Glasgow accent and when I say my first name in my normal way, I'm often not understood. So I had taken to answering the phone in a kind of faux Honor Blackman voice, which Edwyn revelled in mimicking back to me. He still does, in fact, and now Will has joined in with the mockery.

A few weeks later as Trudi recapped for Edwyn on the baseline assessment she had made on her first visits, and compared it to how he had moved on, the first thing she said was: 'Well, you no longer say "Grace Maxwell" all the time.'

'Thank God.' Said with feeling.

In fact he'd moved on to some interesting new exercises, both mental and verbal. To help with the 'pinning a thought down' exercise that I described before, he would make lists. Constructed sentences were too hard; nouns, verbs, and especially conjunctions had deserted him. But lists could be tried.

One of the first was the members of The Who. Roger Daltrey, Pete Townshend, John Entwistle (The Ox!) and Keith Moon. Not necessarily in that order, but over and over again, dozens and dozens of times a day. Sometimes he needed prodding to complete the set, sometimes not. Then, when he had mastered The Who, on to David Crosby, Steven Stills, Graham Nash, Neil Young. Then to pronounce Creedence Clearwater Revival and John Fogerty, a much-loved hero of Edwyn's. And, more heroes: Otis Redding, Steve Cropper, Donald 'Duck' Dunn, Booker T, Al Jackson, the house band of the Stax label and their legendary vocalist.

So many of Edwyn's memories and a good deal of his cognitive abilities were lost to him at this time. If he was shown a drawing of three objects: a garden spade, a wheel-barrow and a television for instance, and asked to point to the odd one out, he would struggle. But the Stax house band he could visualise, no problem. Painstaking and slow, with lots of mistakes, but eventually he would perfect the skill of labelling these treasured mental images. Watching and listening as he repeated these names endlessly, you could be forgiven for thinking that this was evidence of him having lost his marbles, somewhat. I never saw it like that. Quite the reverse. I could see exactly what he was trying to do with the lists. Order the jumble, start the process with familiar, talismanic facts. I thought it was a clever strategy and I joined in with him enthusiastically. It was also an example of Edwyn's prodigious work ethic. Everything was absolutely knackering and stamina had to be built up by working him to the point of fatigue – beyond which it was useless, counterproductive even. But Edwyn would will-ingly push himself to the limit.

•

AROUND THE SIX week mark of his hospital stay a lot of things happened at once. After a few prodding phone calls, Edwyn was assessed by a consultant member of the team from the regional rehabilitation unit (RRU) at Northwick Park Hospital in Harrow, north west London. This was to determine his suitability for a place. Not knowing what the criteria were, I approached it a bit like it was an exam we had to pass, trying to second-guess what would tick the correct boxes. This was clearly insane as I had no idea what I was on about, but I think I managed to convey something of my neurosis to Edwyn. I can see him now, concentrating like mad as the doctor asked him various questions, which he couldn't answer, but responded to with ineffable politeness. Even as the guy was writing something in his notes, the penny dropped about a move he had requested Edwyn to make a few moments ago. Too late and unseen by the doctor, he moved his left leg up and down obligingly. I tentatively enquired about the wait and was met by a more or less non-committal answer.

I had also been to see a couple of private rehab units, but only one of them seemed like a good place. It also happened to be the nearest one to us and was situated over two floors in the Wellington Hospital in St John's Wood. Hazel and I met a lovely young man, the administrator of the unit, who showed us around. Very impressed with the set-up, the way the place was organised and the facilities, we sat down to talk turkey with him. He asked me if we had private insurance and I told him we hadn't. He said it probably wouldn't have helped much anyway, as the average policy would give you about two weeks maximum in a facility like this. The average stay of a brain rehab patient is three months.

He went on to ask me if we were on the list for any NHS facilities and when I told him that Northwick Park was the frontrunner, although I had been told that there was a waiting list and a lot of pressure for places, he said, 'As far as I know it's an excellent rehab unit. Fight tooth and nail for Edwyn's place. Coming here for three months under your own resources would probably bankrupt you. Many of our longer-term patients are from overseas and money is no object. For you guys, I would recommend doing your utmost to get Edwyn into Northwick Park and then, if later on you feel we can contribute to the rehab process, come back and talk to us. For now, what we can do is come along to the Royal Free and do an assessment. He sounds like someone who will derive a lot of benefit from intensive rehab.' I was somewhat nonplussed to get such positive and practical support from a private hospital, who I would always have assumed were into taking the money and running. This small unit was almost always operating at full capacity, so I suppose there was no need for the hard sell, but all the same, his good advice and kindness were much appreciated. I practically threw my arms around anyone during those days who reached out to me with kind words and solid help.

•

BACK AT THE hospital, the neurosurgeon came for a look at Edwyn and, looking at the space in his skull, under the skin where the bone used to be, asked me if I could remember where they had kept the bone flap.

Eh?

'I'm pretty sure it's in the fridge, but sometimes we pop it in the abdomen to keep it healthy.'

Sorry?

He had a feel around Edwyn's tummy and nodded.

'Yes, must be in the fridge. Don't worry, it's got his name on it.'

Why had I not thought about the space in his head before now? It had honestly not even crossed my mind that something would have to be done to fill it. Ridiculous of me. It was a pretty sizeable hole. Surgery was scheduled for the early part of the following week.

It was Easter weekend and we had a lot of family visitors, including that first visit from Trudi Jenkins for Edwyn's speech therapy assessment. I remember Will made himself really sick one night at the funfair that always visits Hampstead Heath at Easter. He ate loads of candyfloss and went on the worst, most rickety, fastest ride about eight times with our next-door neighbour, Alex. Then, of course, threw up, horribly. I carted them both home, listening to Alex's lurid description of flying sick, as Will insisted how totally it had been worth it.

•

ON TUESDAY 29 March, two women from the Wellington came to make their assessment of Edwyn at lunchtime, which went well, and just as they were finishing, the theatre porters arrived to wheel him off for surgery to replace the bone flap. It was all a little hurried, getting him out of there, so neither of us had time to worry. But he was gone for several hours, longer than I had been led to believe it would take. Eventually Greg, the Jarvis Cocker lookalike staff nurse, took pity on my fidgeting and corridor stomping and called down to find out what the score was.

'He's all done. Back soon, don't worry.'

Edwyn reappeared in a very groggy state, with a freshly shaved head, a neat row of staples in his long wound and his skull complete. The next few days were for gentle recuperation. But he felt miles better by the following day and able to get up for a little physio. At this time that consisted largely of him being hauled to his feet by two therapists and held there for thirty seconds. He had even had a session inside a standing frame contraption, a pivoting stretcher, which, true to form, he loathed. But I could well appreciate the importance of reacquainting his body with gravity, no matter if it made him feel tired and a bit queasy.

FROM THE THURSDAY to the Tuesday morning, Edwyn didn't leave his bed. The ward was very short staffed and I was not confident enough at this time to get him up by myself.

On Thursday 31 March I was stopped dead in my tracks when Greg called me over to say that Northwick Park had been on the phone. A place had opened up. We'd be on our way next Thursday, 7 April. I was absolutely ecstatic. Edwyn was slightly confused by my crazed reaction.

135

'Seven days, love, only seven days. You're moving on. We're going to get you better!'

Of course it hardly seemed possible that it could really be happening. And it wasn't. Just when you think you've pulled all the strands of a plan together ... We were both about to get the stuffing well and truly knocked out of us. On that weekend, I'm so glad I could not foresee what was around the corner. I needed the surprise element of the forthcoming events to supply the adrenalin rush that would re-energise me for yet another fight ahead.

•

ON TUESDAY MORNING, two days away from our big move to rehab, and on what had seemed like a normal ward day after a quiet Monday, Edwyn was helped out of bed and supported in a standing position by two physios. After about a minute all the colour had drained from his face. He was passing out. Peculiarly, a large swelling had rapidly developed around his left eye. Back in bed, the colour returned, but the swollen eye remained. Instantly, a small team gathered around him. Edwyn had a high temperature. The doctor prescribed penicillin. I interrupted to remind them that he was allergic to penicillin.

'He's had it before with no ill effects,' the doctor answered, a bit miffed with my interference.

Fortunately one of the excellent nurses, Mary, was in attendance.

'He did react, actually. A bad rash.'

Good grief, I remembered that rash, early on in the stroke unit, all over the groin and abdomen. They had given him penicillin in spite of it being in his notes that he was allergic. I had had no idea. But I was too preoccupied with the ongoing drama to get into a retrospective battle right now. Another antibiotic was prescribed and we monitored him all day. I could feel my growing panic that our window of opportunity to transfer to Northwick was slipping away.

By the next day Edwyn seemed a bit better. The swelling around his eye was less, but around his scar line, a large arc, where his staples had been removed, and over his left temple area, there was a suspicious redness. However, the consensus seemed to be that he merely had a reaction under the skin, the temperature was abating and the move was still on. Thank goodness. We had seen several infections come and go and I was sure he was seeing this one off as he had all the others.

That day and night I took a few pictures of Edwyn with his favourite nurses and packed away his belongings. I had a list of his requirements for the new hospital, which came in a lengthy introduction booklet they had sent Edwyn. Very exciting. I said goodbye to the night staff and tucked Edwyn in with the promise of a red-letter day to come on the morrow.

THE NEXT MORNING, Thursday 7 April, I arrived trundling a suitcase full of things Edwyn would need at the new

137

hospital and packed away his few toiletries. I had a cake, a card and some presents for the ward. Were we really moving on? I couldn't believe the sense of anticipation. Soon the transport guys arrived and it was time to say goodbye. We took our jubilant leave of the staff on Berry Ward, many of them instructing Edwyn that the next time they saw him they expected to see him walk onto the ward. Then we were downstairs, Edwyn experiencing fresh air for the first time in seven weeks. I can't say he liked it much as it was a freezing day and the cold air hit him like a shock. But the drive to Harrow he did enjoy. Even from his recumbent position in the back of the ambulance he could see trees and blue sky and we were kind of half-singing together, which seemed to bemuse the young transport guy who sat beside us. These guys are not paramedics, more like porters who drive, and our two were quite rough characters. It was a funny journey. I was finding everything hilarious. I think I may have been a little hysterical.

On arrival at Northwick Park, we made our way to the RRU, as the unit was always referred to, and Edwyn was pushed into a room with three other guys to begin the long-winded process of booking in. We went through a great many introductions, from his named nurse and his physio, to the registrar – a bright, pleasant woman. Edwyn was examined and after a bit of to-ing and fro-ing, the doctor returned and said that she was concerned because he had spiked a temperature and she could see the redness at his temple. She asked me how it looked today compared to yesterday? I thought it looked about the same. By the time Hazel arrived later in the afternoon, Edwyn had been examined by a neurosurgeon and I'd been told that the unit was very unhappy about accepting him at this time, when he was showing signs of a post-operative infectious complication, something they were not equipped to deal with. One of the requirements of rehab units is that patients are medically stable and therefore fit for therapy. I felt like begging them to give it a day or two. Utter desperation, I know, but the thought of going back ...

By early evening, after a flurry of phone calls, it was definite. Edwyn was to be sent back. A fair bit of argy bargy was clearly taking place between the doctors at both hospitals. The Northwick Park team were clearly annoyed that he had been discharged to them with an infection. There was now no bed for Edwyn at the Royal Free. It was eventually agreed he would stay at Northwick Park for the night and return to the Royal Free in the morning, when a bed would be found.

Edwyn looked so crestfallen. Hazel and I tried to hide our blank disappointment from him. I reassured him we would be back on the rehab unit within the week, that they would hold his place for him here. Later on, I gave him a hug and left him alone in this unfamiliar place that was chucking him out in the morning. I walked off down the corridor with Hazel, pulling my big stupid case behind me, too desolate to even cry. I went home to bed where I lay rigid with anxiety most of the night.

•

WHEN I CALLED in the morning, the transport was already on its way for him.

'Which ward is he going to?'

'Oh, they don't have one yet, so he'll go to A&E to begin with.'

No. No. No.

The anger balled inside me and I could barely see straight as I called the main switchboard at the Royal Free and asked to be put through to the neurosurgeons. I got a secretary. I asked to speak to Edwyn's consultant, who was, of course, unavailable. I passed a detailed message along to him via the secretary that consisted of a set of instructions as to what should happen to Edwyn on his arrival back at the hospital, none of which was up for negotiation. I stressed how seriously my message had to be taken, for given the choice between the hassle of sorting out a proper bed for Edwyn on a proper ward, or dealing with the fall-out I could promise would ensue, they definitely wanted to go for the former option. I was precisely that person that hospital trust executives fear most; a righteous, angry relative with a potential hotline to the media. As time went on, I would become aware that hospital bigwigs have an absolute horror of negative publicity. I had no intention of dealing with Edwyn's private ordeal in public, but occasionally the unspoken threat was enough.

I hung up and high-tailed it to Hampstead, accompanied by Elaine, my sister-in-law, who had arrived from Scotland the previous evening with David and my nephew Ricky. On arrival we rushed to the A&E department, to see if he had arrived. No sign. As we came towards the lifts en route for the neurosurgery floor (I'd been told he definitely couldn't go back to his old ward), there he was, on a trolley, being pushed into a lift. From one glance I could tell how fraught his morning had been. The world was disorientating at the best of times for Edwyn. The return journey must have been lonely and scary, because he was very relieved to see me. This was Elaine's first sight of Edwyn since he had fallen ill. As practical as she is compassionate, she was thankfully unfazed by this dramatic introduction to our new world.

Edwyn was returned to the neurosurgery ward where he had been on all those weeks ago. His temperature was still up and he seemed a bit less well than the previous day, and I tried to put that down to all the upheaval. We were placed in a four-bed bay, where his cell mates were all very unwell people. Two of them were very vocal, not uncommon on a neurosurgery ward. My heart was always full for these souls, and I certainly felt a kinship with their families, but it can be quite an alarming thing to be around if you're not used to it. As for Edwyn, he had simply had enough and was letting me know it in no uncertain terms. Each time a patient would begin making a lot of noise, he would voice his despair. In spite of his lack of access to words, Edwyn was always quite brilliant at getting his message across. He was frustrated, unsettled and afraid. I was at my wits' end. What to do?

His consultant came to see him and we had a chat. He confirmed that Edwyn had an infection in the wound area, but was hopeful that it would clear up in a few days. That was at least something to hold on to. We could get back to the RRU as planned within the week. Meanwhile, was there any chance we could get him a private room? I had asked Edwyn if he wanted me to do this, and the answer was a definite yes. Anything for some peace.

So that was how we fetched up on the top floor of the hospital late that night – a bonus being that his move had freed a ward bed – for what I thought would be a few quiet days' recuperation. After all, with Edwyn's track record, this thing would be shrugged off with a short course of antibiotics. Relentless positive thinking.

Of course, my optimism was to be short-lived. Our venture into the world of private medicine, as provided in NHS hospitals, would prove to be a disastrous move on my part, lasting not days, but seven long weeks.

Edwyn's memories are different. This was a time of quiet for him, as he was left untroubled, except by me, for hours at a stretch, in the peace of his room, silently trying to make sense of himself.

'Calm and tranquil.'

These are the words he chose many months later to describe his feelings as the days turned to weeks on the ward which would all but reduce me to a wreck.

It had begun on the evening we arrived. I went in search of an extra pillow to support Edwyn's arm and shoulder.

No spare pillows, I'm afraid.

What, nowhere in the hospital?

We only have our own supply.

It's only a pillow, for goodness sake. Shall I go and get one? I'm sure his old ward would give me one. If it's such a big deal I'll bring my own in tomorrow.

A great sigh. Ten minutes later a pillow appears.

Every little thing in this joint would be this hard.

•

ENTIRELY BY ACCIDENT, I discovered that Edwyn had tested positive for MRSA, one of the infections known in the wider world as a hospital superbug, in a passing remark I overheard the following day. I tried to find out more. No doctors being around, because it was Saturday, all I could ascertain was some half-baked, evasive stuff about how it may simply be a case of the bug being present on his skin as opposed to a systemic infection. Which means it's in the bloodstream. Hmm. Dubious. Alarm bells were beginning to ring. Nothing else could be gleaned until Monday.

In true Dunkirk spirit, we gathered in Edwyn's spiffy private room on that Saturday afternoon, ready to watch the Grand National. I'm one of those types who has one bet a year on the daftest race it's possible to bet on. It's a family tradition. We all do it in memory of my dad. It was a thing in our house when we were kids, and he would put sixpence each way on for all of us (that comprehensively dates me!). I won once, about thirty bob, on a rank outsider. When I introduced Edwyn to the custom in the mid 80s, he rather startlingly won on his first attempt, with a horse called West Tip, if memory serves me. This Grand National day, David had placed bets for the lot of us, including thirteen-year-old Ricky and his big cousin Will, and we watched as not a single one of our horses even made a place. I doubt if many made it home. Never mind, we had a good laugh and the bonus of the afternoon was that much needed haircut for Edwyn, courtesy of Elaine. She had been a hairdresser in her earlier life, when David and she first met and, as I reminded Edwyn of the salon she had run in my home town all those years ago, he suddenly piped up: 'Tangles!'

The mind is such a junkyard. The memories that surface are so ridiculously random. I would never have remembered the shop name.

•

RICKY'S REACTION TO seeing his uncle for the first time since his illness was very stoical, mirroring his Will's attitude. Edwyn and Ricky had a very funny relationship with each other, based on Edwyn being an idiot uncle to him and his older brother, Jake.Both of them lapped it up. Here is a typical sketch:

Driving along in Caithness, near our home in the far north of Scotland, I looked across to a field and saw something odd. One cow on top of another. Not a bull and a cow, you understand, but two cows. Stupidly, I pointed out this interesting phenomenon to Edwyn.

'You've never heard of the famous Lesbo Cow of Caithness, then?'

The three boys in the back of the car, aged between nine and thirteen, fall apart laughing. So, of course, he keeps it going. He gives Lesbo Cow a funny, deep voice, not unlike Fenella Fielding with a West Country accent, and gives her a personality, an entire back story. And keeps it up, intermittently, for days. Ricky can still remember all of the charming bedtime stories his uncle fashioned around the life of Lesbo Cow.

On another expedition in the wilds of Caithness, we were visiting one of our regular haunts, a Neolithic burial chamber situated in a very remote place that was, until recently, hardly ever frequented by other people. It's a bit spooky and therefore a good place to take kids. Nowadays, a tourist sign tempts a few strays to it and one day, while we were cavorting around in a very unreverential way, there were a couple of other visitors. They turned out to be German, which we discovered from their accent when they called out sternly to our noisy lads, 'BE QUIET!'

For a moment we were stopped in our tracks. It was really odd to get a school-teacherish Germanic rebuke out here on what we considered to be our turf.

Edwyn broke the silence with a disgusted grunt and, turning to the kids, broke into a stupid dance as he chanted in a stage whisper: 'Two world wars and one world cup!'

Even I was rolling in the heather, creased up laughing.

During a visit to London when Jake was about eight

years old, Edwyn inhabited the character of an alien from the planet Cyclax (a popular brand of women's face cream at the time) for an entire day. Jake became quite attached to the Cyclaxian and they exchanged correspondence for a while.

When Ricky first walked towards Edwyn's bed on the previous evening, while Edwyn was still on the busy ward, I was a little worried for the young lad.

'Ricky.'

'Hiya, Uncle Edwyn.'

'Ricky.'

'What?'

'Ricky.'

'What?'

'Nothing.'

This was an old routine of Rick's. He'd do it to his mum. Call her name, get a response, call again, ever more agitated, until he got her properly worried and then deliver a jaunty 'Nothing!' So it was very reassuring, in these weird and scary circumstances, to see evidence of the old familiar uncle. By Saturday afternoon, Ricky had made the adjustment to the new version of Edwyn in a way that only the young folk can, with no fuss or bother.

We said goodbye to the family on Monday 11 April. I still had not had any luck at having a proper conversation with anyone about Edwyn's infection. He seemed no better, probably a bit worse in fact, by Monday evening. I resolved to pin someone down the next day for some straight talking.

•

WHEN I ARRIVED the next day we had a development. Edwyn's wound had re-opened and was oozing some evil-looking stuff.

Edwyn's consultant came to see him and it took about ten seconds for him to declare that the infected bone flap would have to come out fast. First thing the next morning, in fact. Reeling a little, I asked him what type of infection it was.

'We won't know that until we get results back from the lab.'

More ducking, I suspected.

Edwyn's registrar friend, one of the young doctors who carried out his original emergency surgery, came to see him.

'Sorry about this, Edwyn. You could do without it, I know. But this surgery will be straightforward compared to what you've been through.'

Edwyn smiled and shrugged.

'He's accepting the situation with …' I began

'Equanimity,' Edwyn finished my sentence.

Astonishingly, exuberantly, Edwyn Collins. He can't walk, he can't read or write, he can't talk in sentences, he feels like shit, but he comes up with an absolutely tremendous one-word response. A moment like that can keep you from falling apart, fills you with hope and optimism, energises you. Edwyn always made sure I had sufficiency of these moments to buoy me up.

•

I WAS BACK at his side at dawn the next day.

A rather garrulous anaesthetist came along for a consultation. Most doctors are creatures of few words. I always felt like a right yapper beside them. But this guy was up for a blether. At one point, flicking through the great tome that was Edwyn's medical notes, he remarked, 'There's far too much here for a fit young man of your age. Still, after what has occurred, you're extremely lucky not to have found yourself keeping company in the cabbage patch.'

He actually said that! The smooth-talking bastard.

We didn't mind his rather indelicate style, actually. It was an entertaining diversion on an anxious morning. Edwyn kept pulling faces at me.

So once again I was waving him off to theatre, outside the bed lifts. More hours to kill. The knots in the tummy, the tension in the head and neck, were becoming a way of life. Fortunately, I was brilliant at not dwelling on the detail of what was happening to him. I had perfected the art of the blank brain and strolled off to drink coffee and pretend to read the *Guardian* in Starbucks.

Edwyn was in the recovery room a long time this time, and was still very sleepy behind his oxygen mask when he came back to the room.

He was looked after for the rest of the evening by a very nice, extremely capable Irish nurse who was not a regular on the ward, sadly.

She asked the groggy Edwyn the traditional post-op questions: 'Can you tell me your name?'

'Edwyn Collins.'

'And what's the prime minister's name?'

Would he know this? I wasn't sure.

'Tony Blair.'

'And do you like him, Edwyn?'

'No.'

She looked up at me, laughing.

'He's doing just great!'

•

NEXT MORNING, EDWYN was fully awake and aware. His head once more in a big bandage, I noticed that there seemed to be a large amount of blood clotted in his hair and even at the back of his neck. His doctor reassured me that the surgery had gone just fine.

'We gave him a thorough irrigation, a good clean out. That's the bone flap gone for good. When he's better, he'll have a scan to measure him up for a personalised titanium plate, which he'll have fitted later in the year. He'll have to be very careful of any falls in the interim, while his brain is unprotected in that area.'

As I absorbed the significance of this for his therapy outlook, I remembered suddenly to ask the killer question.

'The infection, is it MRSA?'

'Yes, I'm afraid so. We'll start him today on intravenous antibiotics. He'll have them once a day.'

'For how long?' Still thinking about therapy and that place at the rehab unit.

149

'Hard to say. Could be a couple of weeks.'

'And do they work?'

'Usually. If they don't, there is one other we can try.'

Oh, hell.

So that was it then. We were stuck here with no chance of an early escape. His place on the RRU at Northwick Park would definitely not be held. Everything was slipping. I had been told and had read everywhere that the chances of a good recovery from Edwyn's type of brain injury depended upon early, intensive, therapeutic intervention, so I had had a dramatic sense of urgency for many weeks. Here we were at week eight with no end in sight.

And, worst of all, we had this dread infection to battle. I was to discover how rife it was in hospitals. Every ward had its MRSA room, or rooms. I had great faith in Edwyn's immune system to cope with infection, but I realised this would be trickier than usual.

I had developed a nasty habit of grinding my teeth. I kept catching myself doing it with such ferocity I feared the onset of lockjaw.

•

WE WERE TO serve out our sentence on this smartly appointed, at least on the outside, private ward. However, looking closer, I really felt we were in a prize dump. This place was a piece of work and a half. Edwyn was never anywhere else in his long hospital stay where I felt, indeed knew him, to be less safe. The collection of half-assed, inattentive eejits that staffed the

ward required constant supervision which, not being forthcoming from the glamorous sister – who would not have been
out of place in a *Carry On* film – needed to come from me. I
recall one afternoon, wearily approaching the hordes of staff
gathered at their accustomed positions by the nurses' station,
where they were writing, writing, always writing drivelous
rubbish in the patients' notes. My weariness encouraged me to
sarcasm, asking: 'Can anyone think of the appropriate collec-
tive noun for this scene?'

Blank looks.

'An indifference of nurses, perhaps?'

What an insufferable smart alec, I hear you say. And I
agree, but for me sarcasm has always been my first line of
defence. And it's useful as a pressure reliever.

•

Once I had a vision
And that vision was intense
And if I'm talking like the mystic
Let me say in my defence
I was out for the count
And when I awoke
I was laughing, uncontrollably
As one might at a joke.
~ Out For the Count, 1984

I have a diary of these weeks cataloguing the endless cock-
ups, hairy moments, confrontations. I felt like I was cling-
ing on by my fingertips the whole time we were there. It

very nearly did for me. My entries are terse, unhappy, and reading them takes me back to specific days, certain moments and feelings. This is a snapshot of what life is like for anyone in the same boat. I know my story, or worse variations of it, is replayed in lives of patients and their families every day in thousands of locations across the land.

Reading it back now I find I have one conclusion: Don't get old and don't get sick. Or, at least, only get old if you can manage to stay very healthy and look after yourself. Even if you have great family support, articulate fighters going to bat for you, it's still going to be horrible. In hospital, you will feel sidelined, abandoned, a nuisance, a non person. Maybe not all of the time, but most of the time. I honestly know this to be true.

•

FRIDAY 15 APRIL: Head covered in ooze this morning. Must find out skin protocols for MRSA. Nobody does the same thing twice. What about showering? Needs to have antibacterial stuff on his skin surely?* Checked his notes and found out they forgot to give him Teicoplanin today [Edwyn's IV antibiotic]. What a nightmare. Found out what time all drugs

---

* *Edwyn had been in hospital for two months and had not yet had a shower. My sister the nurse was aghast at this. While he had a trachy wound in his throat it would be tricky, but even so. Manoeuvring a tall, immobile man like him into a shower would be hard work and time-consuming and bed baths were an easier option. There were lots of half-baked excuses offered, but hospital staff are practised at defending the indefensible, like politicians.*

are due so I can check. Meeting with sister about all these things. Said I should check with physio if shower is OK. What? OK, I'll do it. Missed Trudi sesh because of surprise scan which took hours of waiting around downstairs.

•

SATURDAY 16 APRIL: Head left encrusted again this morning. Every effing day this lackadaisical nursing. But Nurse C (a guy) on today, whom Edwyn likes. Helped me get him out of bed and into a wheelchair, a dodgy one. I went searching the hospital for it. They are like hen's teeth and the porters stash them in secret places. We had to fashion a foot rest from a pillow case. Pushed him into the lift and downstairs (with me) for the very first time. Went to front door for a look out at the real world. Hospital is weekend quiet. As we're there, in walks Petra, flown down from Glasgow. To see him there, at the front door, well, floods of tears all round. Go to canteen for a coffee, now he's knackered. Petra has brought a scrapbook,* full of childhood stuff, lots of family letters, especially Grandpa, wonderful thing.

•

MONDAY 18 APRIL: Phoned to check they've changed the dressing after yesterday's cock-up. Got in late because of

---

* At Trudi's suggestion we compiled memory books for Edwyn, full of the significant events, people, places in his life. Unlike Edwyn, I'm not gifted in the visual arts, but I tried. Others, including Petra and Edwyn's Mum, made a lovely job of it.

couch guy, Hazel to the rescue.* Mr B (consultant) says Edwyn will be swabbed daily. Will have to remind them. Ask physio about showering and she looks at me in amazement. Why have I not forced this before?

•

TUESDAY 19 APRIL: I arrive 10.30 am and he's filthy. Covered in stuff. Go in search of a nurse. No sense of urgency to be found so blow my stack with Sister G. I've lost it right now. Hauled her in to look at Ed while I turned my back and stared out the window so they wouldn't see me blubbing.

Anyway, red-letter day, first shower. I helped the nurse and we're in the middle of it when Dr C (neurosurgeon) popped his head round the door. Apologised to Edwyn for intruding and impressed upon the nurse that he has written him up for more regular changes of dressing. Lovely man.

Trudi 6.30 pm. Thank God for Trudi.

•

THURSDAY 21 APRIL: I'm still in the dark. Lots of unanswered questions. The subject of MRSA makes them so cagey and defensive. Either that or clueless. Plumbers started the bathroom.** *S. Times* rang me (how do they

---

* *I was having a collapsed sofa upholstered at home, in readiness for Edwyn's eventual return.*

** *I thought this was a good time to get the builders in! In fact, work was due to begin on making a sort of walk-in shower room just the day after Edwyn got ill. Having put it on hold, I thought it might be a good idea to press on, as I'd need it for his return. Compared to everything else that was taking place, the ordinary chaos of builders in the house was nothing.*

get your no.?) and asked if Ed had MRSA. No comment.*
This is a hard time of going nowhere. Edwyn oozing like
anything. Nobody on it. This ward.

•

FRIDAY 22 APRIL: 3 pm Trudi. 9.30 am appointment
Lee.** Hazel with Ed. He and she great. I come back and
cast my gimlet eye around the room. Hazel to Edwyn:
'Look, Nurse Ratched's back.' [There were more than
enough similarities to *One Flew Over the Cuckoo's Nest* in
that place.]

I tried something – on the headphones Ed heard
'Promised Land' (Johnny Allen) and 'Photograph' (Ringo
Starr) and we both cried and cried.***

---

* *During this time there was an election campaign and MRSA was a*
hot topic. I told Edwyn that although he wasn't very famous, he was
currently the most famous person in the country with the infection. The
hospital press office were very twitchy. One would have thought that
would have translated into ultra attentiveness on the treatment front,
but that would have required much better internal co-ordination than
exists in most hospital trusts. The left hand has not much clue what the
right is up to.
** *My hairdresser and friend. Hazel made the appointment, unable to*
bear any longer the sight of my two-inch roots.
*** *This was the first time Edwyn had felt able to listen to music. He*
had refused to do so up until this day. The CD is one that he had
compiled for the car journey north the previous Christmas. He was quite
overwhelmed as the first notes flooded his ears and cried uncontrollably.
I joined in in sympathy, but also in relief that music, blessedly, could
still have this effect upon him.

Later with Trudi. Talked about music and the brain.* Sang (a snatch of) AGLY ['A Girl Like You'] then together, Granny's Charlie Chaplin song from the First World War. Then, from nowhere, very softly, a verse of 'Out For the Count' [An Orange Juice song from 1984]. (Bit of help). What a day.

Nan came.

Quote of the day**: 'None whatsoever.'

•

SATURDAY 23 APRIL: I'm agitated at everything today. Nan with me. Edwyn not washed or dressed until 1.45 pm. Nan telling me to calm down but I can't. Edwyn is OK with everything. The sister tells me a photographer found lurking outside the ward, so now he is 'John Smith' on the board. Ludicrous.

Quote of the day: 'Subtle differences.'

•

---

* *Trudi described an experiment her dad, a neurologist, had conducted. He scanned the brains of classical musicians whilst they listened to familiar music and the brains of non-musicians whilst listening to the same music. The musicians' brains lit up all over the place while the reaction in the non-musician was very muted by comparison. It would therefore appear that when a musician listens to music, they are having a very different, much more complex experience than a non-musician.*
** *Everyday speech, routine requests, exchanges of information were so difficult for Edwyn, but he did enjoy firing off these little gems occasionally, and I liked recording them.*

SUNDAY 24 APRIL: Sister (not usual one) suggested a 'multi-disciplinary' meeting tomorrow. Fat chance of that happening. (It doesn't.)

Irish grumpy nurse who hates me asks me to leave the room when they're getting Edwyn out of bed to go to the loo. For his privacy. I do as I'm told but am incandescent. Normally I'm left to do all this stuff myself. I come back fuming and Edwyn's laughing at me. In very bad 'Oirish' accent he says, 'Grace Maxwell, feck off.' Ha ha.

•

MONDAY 25 APRIL: Talked to consultant. New antibiotic, fusidic acid, for the bones. Still on IV one. Still oozing but not so much? Talked to sister after they forgot his new ABs [antibiotics] at six o'clock. Hopeless. Tomorrow I meet head of infection control. Trying to see if he can be re-assessed for rehab. Edwyn to the gym. Did absolutely great. Went to get tiles [for bathroom] and had a fight with a traffic warden.

Came back and noticed Ed's canula was out. Not back in until 4.30 pm after I kicked up. So, eight and a half hours late without his IV ABs … this f–king place will do me in.

•

TUESDAY 26 APRIL: Bought a PC for Trudi's software and did a bit more work on the book of his life. Edwyn spikes a temp. He is so patient while I am quietly losing my grip. Pav and Henri with Ed while I met infection control nurse.

Asked about protocols. She explained. Asked about supervision and monitoring. Described inconsistencies. She did that expert stonewalling thing. What's the use of spending months drafting policy you don't implement? One nurse, who took a paper towel to his head, back and forth, I asked why she did that when others approach him with sterile packs. Answer: 'We all come from different countries, you see.' Eh? Told IC nurse this story. Awkward silence.

Quote of the day: 'The situation is evolving.'

•

THURSDAY 28 APRIL: Neuro physio in room with Nadia and assistant. V. clever and exciting. Supporting him (they're strong) and with Nadia's hand firmly in his right-hand butt cheek they step him across the floor.

Missed his drugs again today. They keep telling me he's only on one until I show them his chart. Unbelievable. (Happened yesterday as well.) Still oozing.

•

FRIDAY 29 APRIL: Talk today of more surgery to 'irrigate'. Waiting until Tuesday to decide. Come on Edwyn. Nurse Elvis on the ball. Edwyn loves him. Discovered we could use staff canteen. Food horrible but has nice patio area if it's warm.

•

SATURDAY 30 APRIL: Forgot his drugs again. Apparently it's because it's written on the wrong page of his notes. So I put PTO in big letters. Oh dearie me. Gave Edwyn a beautiful shave. Myra here. Had a lovely visit from John K.* Nipped out for a glass of wine with him. A tonic for the troops.

•

MONDAY 2 MAY: Quiet here, Bank Holiday. Amete came, then Paul and Jeni Cook. Went downstairs with them and Edwyn out into the sunshine. Came back to find Edwyn's room had been robbed. Laptop, Walkman and hair clippers(!) gone. What a place. Nurse G forgot his 2 pm meds and gave me the old flannel. Aaaargh … Will came at night and we had a fight because he's lost his keys again and I'm afraid some toerag has them. So change the locks. Got home 9.30 pm and had three glasses of wine with Vanessa and Sharon.

•

TUESDAY 3 MAY: Edwyn is depressed today. Strange for him. Think he feels stuck. Rehab say they need all clear before he can come back. Bit grumpy with me and listless. Slept loads. The wound is definitely better. No need for surgery. Will came and Ed cheered up when he lay on top of him (his customary greeting to Edwyn)! They watched Liverpool V Chelsea and Edwyn remembered an old 'Chelsea Chelsea' song from the 70s.

•

* *John Kennedy, Edwyn's former lawyer and our good friend. Also the first to suggest this book. Each anecdote I'd tell him would be met with, 'Put it in the book!'*

THURSDAY MAY 5: Nurse A does his dressing like she's scrubbing out a pan with a Brillo pad. Can't watch. Forgot his meds again. I don't even react any more. They've got hides like elephants, this mob. Mum at home. Went to see Frankie and Annette Miller.* Came home v. late to huge amount of roses from John K. Very touched.

Quote of the day: 'Life is an aphrodisiac.' Really, Edwyn?

•

FRIDAY 6 MAY: Left Edwyn alone in a dodgy wheelchair for half a minute and when I came back he was on the floor, chair upended, with a look of horror on his face. Jesus. Got him up and back in the rotten chair God knows how. I wasn't going to ask for help, because it was my fault. How awful, just didn't want to get caught. I was begging him not to let on. He had a small graze on his face. When the nurse saw it I lied, said he bashed against the bed. Old honest injun Ed, the disloyal git, was desperately trying to contradict me and get the real story out. Thank God for aphasia, they couldn't understand him, so I got away with it. He kept pointing at me, with the accusing finger! I blustered on. After they had gone I asked him if he still trusted

---

* *Frankie Miller, a Scottish singer most famous in the US, had a brain haemorrhage in 1994 which ended his career. His wife Annette contacted me early on and despite all they have to deal with daily, she and Frankie have ever since been cheerleaders for Edwyn. Annette, having been through everything imaginable, is a mine of information and support. The first time Frankie and Edwyn met face to face, Frankie put his arm around him and simply said, 'Thank God.'*

me. He said no, very firmly. Got a better chair and pushed him to Starbucks for gigantic cappuccino to make up.

•

SATURDAY 7 MAY: Hazel and Sarah (my niece) had lunch with us but too cold to go out. Had to remind nurse about 2 pm meds AGAIN. Then Will came and we had a laugh. At night, Lee came and gave him a great haircut. I wanted to get her a taxi home and she said no, she'd get the train.

Edwyn: 'I insist.' He was really chatty today, trying hard. His room is full of flowers from the Franz Ferdinand lads, Wet Wet Wet and Harry Hill, and some exotic Japanese fuzzy thing from Seb. Glorious.

•

SUNDAY 8 MAY: Came in at 10.30 am to see Edwyn sleeping peacefully in his chair like an old man. Hurried staff along to get him ready for Trudi at 11.30 am. Nurse Elvis changed his dressing. Wound nearly there now. Went to the Garden Gate (the pub) down the hill for Sunday lunch. This was almost a total success, although Ed was a bit chilly. 'Freezing. Drink up!' Still, our first taste of normality, or it felt like that to me. And I had his duffel coat on him.*

Christmas 2004 I had bought Edwyn a beautiful Dior duffel coat in Selfridges' sale, half price. Still the most expensive coat he's ever had. It was a big hit. After he got ill, I would come home from hospital each night and see it hanging at the bottom of the stairs. Just the sight of it would give me a pang. So how marvellous to see him wearing it again.

And his hat, of course.*

I was looking at his lopsided hair and trying to think of the guy in the Human League who pioneered that style. 'Phil Oakey,' Edwyn pipes up. The things he remembers, mad.

•

TUESDAY 10 MAY: Edwyn is off all antibiotics as of today. He still has the tiniest bit of ooze, but it looks good. Rehab unit to be alerted. Should I be worried? Will they have a place for him? Ed doing more shouting at me, because I keep nagging him to drink water. Needs 2–3 litres a day. It's a struggle.

•

WEDNESDAY 11 MAY: Trudi, who has kindly phoned N. Park (the rehab unit) says the consultant there says they'll definitely have him back within the next two weeks. I do hope so.

I fall asleep and Edwyn takes umbrage and removes his dressing in protest. Good night nurse, bloke, young, does a good dressing. This helps me go home less miserable.

Quote of the day: 'Suffering is ordinary. Suffering is the place he is understanding. Means towards an end.' Not sure

---

* Pushing a frail Edwyn around the hospital with his bandaged head and his thousand-yard stare, looking a bit like Basil Fawlty in the episode about the Germans, we attracted far too many odd looks, so I took to disguising the bandage with a beanie hat. He became so attached to this style he would later insist on sleeping in his hat and only gave up wearing it all day, every day, towards the end of the year.

how pregnant with meaning this is. But it's impressive in the effort it took.

•

THURSDAY 12 MAY: Pub for lunch again. Met a nice stranger called Al with a T-shirt that said: 'I'm Spartacus'. Will came after school.

And Phil Thornalley;* Edwyn really happy to see him.

Quote of the day: 'Different voices come. It rocks my world.'

•

FRIDAY 13 MAY: Lunch in the pub with Hazel and Keith then Trudi at 2 pm and then physio at 3 pm. Phew. Edwyn out of bed for six whole hours. Just back from physio when a woman from the hospital chaplaincy came to see him. I didn't know what to do. Didn't like to be rude but he was knackered. She asked Edwyn if he practised any religion. He wagged his finger at her and said, 'Never you mind!' Short visit.

•

Old friend and fellow record producer, whom we've known since the early 80s. Many Orange Juice records were recorded at the famous Rak Studios in St John's Wood in London, home to Rak Records and headed up by the legendary Mickie Most, whose protégé Phil became. Edwyn learned a lot about the skill of record production from Phil and he produced one of his favourite Orange Juice tracks, 'What Presence?!'

SATURDAY 14 MAY: These are quieter and easier days, counting down [to rehab move]. Nan is here for the weekend and we go to the pub for lunch (again). I just need that blast of shoving him into the real world. We bring him in dinner later from Dominiques* and he settles to watch the *The Dam Busters*** on TV. We have an awkward moment when Edwyn remembers what Guy Gibson's black labrador used to be called before they politically corrected the film.*** He bellows it out, even as I'm trying to smother him. I leave him still watching it in the dark. Hope they remember to check that he could turn it off. Apparently, when I'm not there, he doesn't use the nurse button. He just bellows. Good oh.

•

SUNDAY 15 MAY: After a lovely Sunday lunch in the pub garden, Nan heads for the airport and Will goes off with Hazel. The day is spoiled by an argument with a horror-with-attitude at the nurses' station. Nasty, lazy git. I actually shout. I never do that. I hate leaving Edwyn. Go home

---

One of the places I had been buying Edwyn's meals from for months. I was well known and they were delighted to meet him in the flesh. Same as the Garden Gate. His progress had been followed by the kind staff who were part of my support group when I'd dive out for my medicine, a large glass of red wine.

**Edwyn was obsessed with war planes when he was little. The skill of identifying them in silhouette (even the Luftwaffe ones) came back quite early on. Childhood memories run deep.*

***The n– word, I'm afraid.*

to find Will has been terrorised by Sam. Don't know what to do. After this lovely evening I go to bed and have some nice panic attacks.

·

MONDAY 16 MAY: Man from the stair lift company comes to measure us up for a quote. I'm getting way ahead of myself, but I want to be ready.*

Had a meeting with the head nurse of the trust and ditto the infection control boss. So many things I want to say, but recent weeks have knocked the stuffing out of me and I have no strength to start a crusade. Armies of well-paid, well-meaning management types but the overall impression is one of ineffectualness. Kind of vague people, comfortable with meetings and paper policies and all that, but out of their depth at the sharp end. Ah me.

Hazel came and then we had an early dinner at Dominiques.

Full set of swabs today. And bloods. Waiting with bated breath to hear results. Rang NP [Northwick Park] to prod them on. Should hear after their Wednesday staff meeting.**

---

* When Edwyn moved to Northwick Park rehab, they would aim to release him home for overnight and then weekend visits eventually. I wanted to be prepared.
** If Edwyn's tests came back clear of MRSA on three separate occasions, we were off and running. The one advantage of being in the private ward was that he'd been in isolation all this time and therefore less at risk of cross infection, in theory.

Quote of the day: 'What do you want? A medal?'

And when I told him that there was light at the end of the tunnel:

'Debatable.'

•

TUESDAY 17 MAY: Lunch in the pub. He loves those Thai prawns. Back for physio. I head out to take Will to doc. Turns out to be impetigo. It's ultra infectious, doc says he should stay away from Dad for a few days. My God, he's been lying on top of him. Ach, I'm sure he's fine. On my way back meet Jackson (Seb's alter ego), and Hackett* is in the lift. Good laugh for Ed. He seems so well. I'm sure the infection is going or gone. He has much more energy.

Trudi 6 pm.

Quiet night in. Just waiting.

Quote of the day: 'I think to myself, is it any wonder he's gone mad?'

•

WEDNESDAY 18 MAY: Edwyn tired so lunch in. Hazel comes and persuades him out for coffee,** but just before we go we hear the news that he goes to Northwick Park on Monday. Thank God. Thank God. Phone everyone, I'm so

---

* *Andy Hackett, guitarist. London legend, honest guitar dealer of Denmark Street (that's what it says on the T-shirts) has played with Edwyn since 1997 and is one of his closest friends. Since Edwyn's illness, Hackett has been the Rock of Gibraltar.*

excited. Trudi at 5 pm then Ed and I go for a celebration dinner at the GG (pub). Well, sort of. I'm celebrating. He seems neither up nor down.

He is just so well looking. Will is fine, still taking the tablets.

Mum arrives.

●

** *Sometimes the sheer palaver of getting out and about would defeat Edwyn. It involved a lot of heaving him around, dressing him for the weather, transferring etc and then the hair-raising hurtle down the vertiginous Pond Street. Many of the Royal Free chairs were in a bad way, the footrests would scrape against the pavement, we'd get stuck and crossing the road was often hilarious. I had a downhill backwards policy off the pavement, but the drop was about a foot, involving advanced leverage techniques and necessitating stopping the traffic for a bit. The kindness of strangers was sometimes in evidence, but left to my own devices, I had it down pat. The uphill push back was a tremendous work-out. Between that and the weight loss of the last few months, I was in the best shape I'd been in for years. But somehow, as a fitness video, I don't see it working. And I don't recommend the stress diet.*

And then, of course, there was the issue of the loo. Edwyn was attached to a bag, so I used to contrive a method of concealment, except for the day when the side fell off the bloody chair on a bump in the road and everything fell out. A nice lady helped us get it all back together again.

So, sometimes, he would be a bit reluctant to launch our daily assault on the outside world. But it's difficult to convey how important it was for me to grasp these little slices of near normality. To be outside the hospital with Edwyn, breaking free, represented hope for the future. I needed us to be forging ahead all the time. As I write, this feeling has not changed. I still have a horror of not advancing, of the progress tailing off. I'm so glad and grateful for the potential for change that Edwyn has always displayed.

THURSDAY 19 MAY: William trouble kicks off with a vengeance today [Sam and his family]. Mum in the thick of it. Good gawd.

•

FRIDAY 20 MAY: Speak to Edwyn's consultant. They scan Edwyn to take measurements for the titanium plate for his head which will be made in a lab at University College Hospital and fitted at some point later in the year. Says to be very careful until then (for example, don't drop him out of a wheelchair). Talked to him about the likely causes of Edwyn's stroke and likelihood of recurrence.* He assures me that, following all scans, he can confirm that Edwyn has no underlying vascular disease or aneurysms or any evidence of ongoing problems that might raise their head in the future. His blood pressure will always have to be addressed, that is likely a life-long condition. The answer to the why did it happen question? There is none. Just unlucky. That's it.

We have a lovely pub lunch with Andy H, Seb and Robert. (A friend of twenty years and ex flatmate of Edwyn's.) This a proper celebration, lots of laughs and bangers and mash.

On the way back to the hospital, an incredible thing happens. We get chased by a paparazzi photographer and

---

* This had been troubling Edwyn lately. Could it happen again? I was glad to be able to allay his fears.

his reporter. The photographer runs backwards clicking away and the reporter runs alongside us asking daft questions which we do not answer. Ridiculous.*

·

SATURDAY 21 MAY: This is our last weekend at the Royal Free. Dying to go, slightly apprehensive about what lies ahead. The future beckons.

---

*This was my fault. There had been a few articles in newspapers claiming that Edwyn was fighting for his life, in the grip of MRSA. On his website, where I would from time to time update his followers with news of his progress, I decided to admit that he had had the infection, but was now much better, turned the corner, all that and that far from being close to expiring, we were actually in the pub most lunchtimes, although Edwyn was off the booze, enjoying a nice cranberry and orange juice instead. Later that night I woke from a sleep and sat bolt upright. So stupid. Putting our movements into the public domain. But then I forgot about it. No big deal. So the Sun send a pair to stake out the nearest likely pub and a few days later he was in the news. First exclusive picture of sick guy. Oh well.

I'd had many requests for newspaper interviews by this time. While we've been able to talk about our experiences after a passage of a few years, to the music and arts journalists to whom Edwyn would have given interviews before his illness, the bad-news hounds don't grasp the impossibility of talking to the likes of them when you're in the middle of the worst crisis your family has ever faced. I even had a journalist from a huge circulation daily impress upon me in a letter that it was practically my duty to share all family pain with the world. She then went on to offer a financial inducement. An astonishing insight into the workings of the ambulance-chasing sections of our news media.

169

Edwyn has one of his last exchanges with the lift woman.* We go to the Roebuck for dinner. GG too busy on a Saturday night. Feel very protective of Edwyn as I leave tonight. Then I see the night sky. Blue dusk. Two jet trails have crossed, like a St Andrew's cross, so I decide to read it as a good omen.

•

SUNDAY 22 MAY: Family lunch for the last time for now at the GG. See Ronnie's partner outside the hospital having a fag. (Ronnie, the elderly gentleman who was one of Edwyn's cellmates on the stroke unit.) He says Ronnie is holding his own, but the poor guy looks bowed down. Edwyn is charm itself to him. Mum is so impressed at Edwyn's recent improvement. Bed him down for the last time here.

•

MONDAY 23 MAY: We leave the Royal Free at 1.30 pm. Big send off – not. I think the staff on this ward may be very

---

* *The lift voice would chant 'Going up!' and the voice would go up too ... and then 'Going down' with a descending note. In packed lifts, Edwyn used to echo her, a perfect imitation of her singsong voice, usually provoking a weird discomfiture in our fellow travellers. I knew this because of the way they would pretend not to notice what he was doing and nobody would make eye contact with me. I would try very hard not to laugh. You just knew what they were thinking. Spot the loony. So, eventually, I joined in with him and we both copied the lift woman. Two loonies.*

glad to see the back of us. Well, me. Not Edwyn. I don't give a backward glance.

At Northwick Park, Edwyn is given a room on his own while he waits for the superbug all-clear. It's hotter than hell in the RRU, thanks to a lovely early summer heatwave. I'm not allowed to touch him here. Rules. Edwyn not happy. After a bit of negotiation I'm allowed to take him to the cafeteria for a coffee. With the seat belt on.

Quote of the day: 'Get me out of here.' Shit. We've just arrived.

•

TUESDAY 24 MAY: Edwyn even more unhappy. Here we go. I get to take him downstairs, but I'm not allowed to do transfers,* in case I'm dangerous. I have to pass a test first. He's furious now. Wants to go back to the Royal Free immediately. I explain he's here to get therapy which will get him home, but he's having none of it. Implacably opposed to being here. Please help him survive this.

I can't breathe it's so hot. All the radiators are on full blast, locked on. I even brought a spanner to try and knock the thing off. No joy. Sister says they have asked, warned that all the patients will soon be on drips for dehydration. But it's on until the end of May, regardless of the weather.

---

*Getting him out of bed and into a wheelchair. It didn't matter that I'd been doing it for ages, I may have been doing it all wrong and in a way that encouraged bad habits. They could be right, but it's hard not to resent this sudden brake on our activity and on our hard-fought freedom.

Eh? Entire hospital boiling. Honest to God, this stuff kills me. So I call the press office.* Heat off by close of play. Staff amazed.

We meet Pip, Ed's speech and language therapist and also key worker. Ed and she hit it off immediately. Phew, a positive.

•

MY REGULAR DIARY entries end here. I wonder why I stopped? I'm not sure, but here's one theory. Edwyn was now 'medically well', a requirement of rehab. All that remained now was to tackle walking, talking, planning, personal care, reading, writing – all issues of independent living. Straightforward. Although Edwyn was so unhappy, I was somewhat easier in my mind about risks to his health. His safety was no longer an issue. I no longer felt the need to keep a contemporaneous note, as my lawyer calls it, in case I needed to call the guilty to account. Also, I was pretty exhausted by the end of our stay at the Royal Free. It had been a long haul. I don't think I could face writing my endless moaning misery down any more. Life was simply

---

* *The press officer's first response was, 'I think you've got the wrong department.' My experiences in the Royal Free had taught me that if they are involved, things move fast. If you have reached the end of your rope, or if you just need to cut to the chase, the trick is: always call the press office. This is the only department in any large organisation that can make everybody jump. Also who know who the responsible people are. A veiled threat is all it takes. It helps, of course, to have right on your side.*

about waiting now, and working for the day he would come home for good. It was a long way off, but come it must.

•

W<small>E WERE EMBARKING</small> upon a war of attrition on the RRU. Edwyn wasn't there a day that he didn't loathe. I hated it too and longed for the day when he would be home. Sometimes the quality but mainly the quantity of the therapy failed to live up to expectations, but I was out of my depth. To stay for the duration or to go home to what? We needed to give it a chance. I was suspending judgement for a while. But, my goodness, how Edwyn hated it.

His stay began with a series of baseline assessments, lasting several days. Edwyn was seen by his physiotherapy team, his speech and language team, his occupational therapist, a neuro-psychologist and his named nurse, an individual who would take overall responsibility for assessing his nursing needs and coming up with a plan for this. This person was Edwyn's least favourite character in his entire hospital stay. She had an unfortunate manner, very patronising, and was sadly lacking in the warmth and empathy department. She had an annoying catchphrase which Edwyn's future roommate Mark identified. When presenting one of the unit's more abstruse regulations, we would look at her in disbelief, and she would say, singsong style, 'Shall I tell you *why?*' I put the fixed grin on but Edwyn was implacably hostile to her.

On the subject of leadership on the unit – doctors. This unit was extremely well served in this department, boasting not one, but three consultants, including a professor, who

founded the unit in the early 90s. It had a top-notch reputation, based on a plethora of published results and peer
papers on the subject of the rehabilitation of those who
have experienced an injury to the brain. I was never too
clear as to how three consultants filled their day on this
unit, but I think the answer lies in the volume of academic
work they produce. And this in turn leads to a great deal of
meetings, courses, planning, evaluating, reporting, data
amassing and analysis. I am not saying there is no value in
all this stuff, but I do think they overdid it in there, on a
grand scale. In the three months Edwyn was in the RRU, I
never met the professor and barely saw the other two, nice
guys that they were.

Conversely, for the duration of our stay, there were
quite serious staff shortages on the therapy side, and many
of Edwyn and other patients' sessions were taken by unac-
companied students. Most of them were very good and I
would never have objected to Edwyn's therapy being part
of a training regime – it's imperative. But students were
definitely used to cover the lack of qualified therapists.

Once again a full history was taken of Edwyn's life
before his haemorrhages, something I had been through
several times. Included were questions about his drug
and drinking habits. I responded with my usual, truthful
answers. He has never smoked. He probably drank more
than was good for him. They asked me how much. He
could drink a bottle of wine in a day without much difficulty. But not every day. (Later this would appear in his
notes as a bottle of spirits a day. Doing that just once would

have *killed* him.) Given his background in the rock business, doctors invariably looked at me with ill-concealed scepticism when I would tell them he's not a drug taker. He's not. It's just a matter of fact. Neither he nor I are prudish about drug use. On this occasion when I am asked the question: 'Was he a recreational drug user?' Edwyn is in attendance and alert. As usual, I answer in the negative, and straight away he pipes up: 'No, that's not true, Grace. Cocaine, I think.'

I look at him blankly. 'When was your coke habit, then?'

'No, I did it. Cocaine.' Firmly.

I wrinkle my brow at him in consternation.

On a handful of occasions many years before, when drunk at parties, I have seen Edwyn dab a damp finger on a line of cocaine and, because he could never bear to shove anything up his nose and has never mastered inhaling, rub it on his gums, like the dentists used to do. I didn't think it merited a mention. He's hardly a drug fiend. This is a man who has never, ever, in his life purchased drugs. But one glance at the doctor told me that I would now be down in the file as an unreliable witness. Anything I said now would be seen as furious back-pedalling from a practised liar. I give up.

•

TO GIVE AN idea of Edwyn's condition at this point, three months after falling ill, these assessments painted an interesting picture.

On the physical side, he was still unable to walk. He

could stand, supported, for a minute, but not really bear weight on his affected right side. When lying down he could draw his right leg up, but within a second or two the right knee would flop over. His right shoulder, arm and hand were relaxed, completely inert. His face had recovered some of its symmetry, but there was still a lack of expressiveness on the right-hand side and also a lack of sensation, causing him to dribble a little on that side. Edwyn had become better at managing this himself though. He also had vision problems, much improved from the early weeks, but his peripheral vision loss on the right was quite marked. The assessment claimed he had continency problems, but I disagreed. If you answered his summons in time, there was no problem. His problem was mobility. Mostly nurses didn't get there with any sense of urgency. Very frustrating, as this is a huge issue of decency and dignity.

On the speech and language and also the cognitive front, the picture is always more complicated. Because Trudi was formerly head of speech and language on this unit and knew everyone in the department, she was able to pass her notes on, which was an enormous help. I also had the reassurance of knowing that when we finally brought Edwyn home, we would be reunited with Trudi and that she would continue to work her magic. In the meantime, he was under the care of Trudi's very able successor, Pip, whom he got on with like a house on fire.

Edwyn's speech had certainly improved a great deal from the early days, but he was still severely aphasic. Word finding was very difficult. He would run into the sand almost immediately. In spite of his eloquent quotes, which would suddenly burst forth when you were least expecting them, speech on demand was still extremely difficult. Getting started was very hard. He would get locked on a word or phrase and repeat it over and over again. It drove him mad. He had some stammering and some trouble with forming words, but this was less severe. In fact, he was the soul of politeness, often pronouncing his hard-won words with exquisite diction. Full sentences were sporadic, rare even. To deliver a narrative, impossible. We have a long shared history, and this, with my familiarity with Edwyn's aphasia and exposure to his new style of communication, meant that I was a pretty good translator and expander of his meaning, although I also struggled. I favoured various techniques. Process of elimination was one, not without its annoyances for both of us. It could drag on a bit. Writing things down was completely out. Even drawing a picture would have been very hard as his left hand was quite unco-ordinated too at this time.

A great deal of the time, Edwyn was pretty quiet. Our conversations could be fairly one-sided, in spite of my efforts to draw him out. At the time, this worried me a lot, but as I reflect on it, and following discussions I have had with him about this period, it would seem that his verbal recovery began in silent contemplation. It was hard to tell at the time what, if any, mental activity was going on behind the wordlessness. It now seems that there was a huge amount happening and that much of it was conscious effort. His previous self, introspective, creative and, very importantly, *productive*, was being employed to great effect. He was, to an extent, healing himself from the inside out.

The dyspraxia was still a problem too. But here we were in rehab, and it was to be addressed. Edwyn's nurses were issued with written instructions about how to cue him whilst teeth brushing. Verbal cues, accompanied by physical demos, but encouraging him to work out the sequence of moves. I arrived on day three to find his face awash with shaving nicks.

'Who shaved you? They've made a right arse of it.'

He shrugged a 'Don't know.' Then, with a laugh, 'Oh, oh, me!'

At this time I wouldn't have let him shave for fear of laceration. I was obviously being over-cautious, because of course it was a good thing to let him try. A few more attempts and he'd improved his technique.

The neuro-psychologist was up next. After a long session she pronounced Edwyn to be suffering from clinical depression. I immediately felt uneasy about this. He was certainly unhappy since his arrival on the unit, and every fibre of his being craved to be home, but I thought this was an indication of excellent mental health. Edwyn had had a stroke, a huge interruption of his mental and physical abilities and had been incarcerated in a place he hated. He was royally pissed off. That is not the same thing as being depressed. She suggested that we started him on the antidepressant *du jour*. 'We've been getting very good results with Zombielobotin [or some such],' she announced brightly. I'm an idiot with no medical qualifications, but I was most wary of using mood-altering drugs, unless strictly necessary. He was always up for therapy, alert, raring to go. I wanted him to stay that way. The yawning chasms of boredom in between were what troubled him. Edwyn was ambivalent about more medication, but when the doctors advised that antidepressants could increase the risk he was under of suffering seizures, Edwyn firmly declined the drugs.

•

AFTER A NUMBER of days, Edwyn's new rehab routine was established. He got the all-clear on the MRSA front and moved into a room with three other guys. He had a therapy timetable pinned to the wall. It seemed a bit sparse to me, considering this was meant to be a centre for *intensive* neuro rehab, but I was told it was important not to overtire him early on. Hmm. This paucity of therapy would turn out to be the major complaint of all the inmates and their families.

Edwyn's biggest moan was reserved for the unearthly time that he was woken up. 6.30 am or 6.45 am, every single day. For him, horrific. This was a man who, before the stroke, had cunningly contrived a life full of interest and activity, but with all of it taking place after midday. The justification for the ghastly early rise was the enormous workload for the nurses, who had to have the patients ready for therapy, which began at nine. All of them required full assistance in the morning and all rehab procedures had to be adhered to, which was time-consuming. However, once you were showered, shaved and dressed, there would be a gap until breakfast at eight and then, depending on your schedule, endless hours of sitting up in your chair, waiting for an appointment, of which some days there might only be two.

Visitors were banned until the end of the therapy day, usually 4 o'clock. By the time I arrived Edwyn would be climbing the walls. He was entirely marooned in his wheelchair, unable to read or use a Walkman. Television just annoyed him as he found most of it difficult to follow. He couldn't get at it anyway, as he had been banned from 'punting' – moving his chair along with his left foot (he ignored this injunction). His room-mates all had electric wheelchairs, but Edwyn had been considered too unreliable for these. With a note of derision, he deduced: 'Because I'm a moron.' His named nurse, the hate-figure for Edwyn, explained to me why he could not have one: 'I'm afraid not, we value our feet and ankles too much.'

•

I'VE BEEN ASKED if Edwyn's long stay in hospital (he was there, all told, for six months) institutionalised him as it does many people. Not a chance. Whilst wrestling each day with his discontent, I rejoiced in his refusal to take any of the rules and regulations lying down, to keep fighting for his release, aware that to kick against the pricks was to be vital and alive, sane and sensible.

But whilst all else was hateful, Edwyn was always keen as mustard for his therapy sessions and threw himself into all that was asked of him. One day I arrived to find an agitated Edwyn trying to tell me something very important. Clearly angry, he repeated: 'Red T-shirts! Red T-shirts! Pip!' Baffled, I went in search of illumination. I found Pip and she explained that he had missed his nine o'clock appointment with her assistant this morning as he was not yet washed and dressed. The red T-shirts referred to the nurses (there was a red and a blue team, wearing coloured shirts to identify them). Pip came back to Edwyn's bedside to finish the story. Apparently, infuriated that he'd been overlooked and missed his appointment, Edwyn had continuously bellowed, 'Red T-shirts!' until all and sundry were alerted, and an apology was forthcoming. Pip was tremendously impressed with the determination of a deeply aphasic man to exact justice, and serve notice on those who thought that because of his limited powers to protest he could be overlooked. It never happened again. He got first shower whether he liked it or not!

●

EXAMINING EDWYN'S TIMETABLE I noted a session called 'Standing Group'.

'What exactly goes on in this one, Mark?' I asked his cell mate opposite.

'Three guesses,' he answered dryly. 'It's not downhill skiing.' Mark's speech had not been affected by his stroke, nor his highly developed sarcasm. A kind of Jack Dee of the RRU.

'What, so you just stand up for forty-five minutes? What the hell does Edwyn do?'

'Well, he's got this wooden frame they trap him in

which stops him from falling over. The rest of us are leaning on the wall bars [they were further advanced than
Edwyn] until we're tired, then you have a bit of a rest, then
up again. Thrilling, really.'

One look at Edwyn's grimacing face said it all. I never
saw him in this contraption, but months later I saw another
man use it, until they had to rescue him from the thing
before he passed out. Edwyn tells me he felt the same. A
horrible but necessary evil if he was to walk again.

•

'CELL MATES' RAYMOND, Fred, Steven and Edwyn would
be compadres, sometimes uneasy ones, for almost the entire
duration of his stay. They had all had strokes, although
Edwyn was the only one who had been through surgery.
Steven was in his late forties and also had speech difficulties.
He was a bit of a loner, a bit of a night owl, loved his football and liked a good curse now and again.

Raymond was in his mid-fifties and had lived in
London for about thirty years, after he came out of the
army where he'd seen active service in the Congo, which
had unfortunately left him with a racist streak. Not virulent
– the casual variety, but eye-watering nonetheless. He had
worked in a factory off the A4 for donkeys' years and, an
unmarried man, was hugely attached to his factory and
workmates. And Mark, the same age as me, forty-seven,
was an accountant who used to work for the MOD. He
was a Led Zeppelin aficionado, obsessive even, and had
named his first son after Jimmy Page. His second little boy

was only four or five and was missing his dad. Everyone had a story.

On the morning after Edwyn's arrival (a Saturday, so no therapy, and I was allowed in early) I came in to a somewhat subdued atmosphere. I breezed about, yacking away and enquired as to whether Edwyn had been behaving himself, something inane like that.

'Well,' replied Mark, in mock exasperation, 'eight o'clock this morning, we're having breakfast, it's a bit quiet and he pipes up, "Boring morons!" I mean, I'm eating me cornflakes, what's he expecting, dancing girls? That's charming, isn't it? "Boring morons." Don't hold back, Edwyn, tell us straight.'

'Oh, sorry, Mark, nasty of me ...' Edwyn was giggling.

The ice broken by a lovely insult, Edwyn was welcomed to the fold and as hard as it is to live in close proximity to three other men, I still think it was infinitely preferable to miserable isolation. And there was shared humour, at least.

Weeks later, after I'd been cleared for car transfers and could take Edwyn out in the evenings, we were off and running every night. The nursing staff found this slightly disconcerting as we were the only consistent nightly absentees – hospital dinner avoiders as ever – and felt constrained to issue me with instructions regarding Edwyn's care. Apparently Edwyn's urine production and bowel movements were strictly monitored and I should be part of this if we were to continue with our skiving-off from the ward routine. I was introduced to something called the Bristol Stool Chart. There really is such a thing. I was desperately trying not to catch Mark's eye as he made mad faces behind the nurse as she explained it, and I assumed a serious expression as I looked at my copy of this odd document. (I considered reproducing it here but thought better of it … If interested, Google it, it's there in all its glory, types 1 to 7.) I overheard a nurse discreetly ask Mark a question one night, in hushed tones. His answer came loudly: 'Yes, thank you nurse, medium soft!'

I was choking.

Edwyn and I returned from a night out once and as I was tucking him in he was struggling to ask me something. Eventually he got it out: 'Bertie Bassett!'

'Oh right. Sorry love, I've left them in the car. I'll bring more tomorrow.' We'd been eating liquorice allsorts on the way back to the hospital, I explained to Mark.

'Oh thank Gawd for that, I thought it was your secret code …'

On the day that the Olympics were announced for London in 2012 I was trying to think of which sport I could take up in time to be part of them. After all, I reasoned, I'd only be fifty-four.

'I know, beach volleyball!'

Cue ungentlemanly groans all round. A right bunch of charmers.

⸱

ON THE FIRST Saturday, having done a reccy of downtown Harrow by car, I asked if I could wheel Edwyn there; I wouldn't have known how to get him into the car at this stage even if I'd been allowed to. The nurses were fine about us going and gave me directions on foot. I think back to the sight of us, me propelling Edwyn alongside a dual carriageway, crossing it via an underpass and then toiling along for another mile or so. How much we must have hated the confines of hospital to do battle like this. Like Lou and Andy from *Little Britain*. Scarily like them, in fact. Me, gassing away, nineteen to the dozen, Edwyn grunting the odd assent. We had a meander and then heaved our way back again. The following Saturday, with my brother David to do the pushing, we discovered Harrow had a Nandos and that it was quite easy to manoeuvre our way around in there. That is what really sold a place to me back then. Access. We had our first dinner out since his arrival and then shoved him back to hospital again.

•

HOW MANY WEEKS would it be until we got the promised home visits at weekends? I was dreaming of them. Edwyn was convinced they were non-existent, a cruel trick played on him by me. I think he thought I'd had him confined to a home for the long-term addled, from which there was no escape.

HOME AGAIN

ON A PERFECT day in early June, I proved him wrong. Edwyn came home. Only for one lovely hour, but he was home, and he knew that one day soon, he'd be home for good.

It had been brewing for a few days. I had been agitating for the home visit to happen as soon as it possibly could. These visits were the preserve of the occupational therapists and they would be assessing everything as they went along. Not just how Edwyn handled it, but me too. And our house, which they would have to visit. Could Edwyn cope with it, would it work? What adaptations would we need? All these tests would have to be passed. There is a side of me that would start a fight with my shadow, but on this day I was a woman with but a single thought. Get him home. I aimed to please. So anxious was I in advance to pass with flying colours I'd tried to pre-empt all the requirements that would be asked of me. So, I had the stair lift installed. I'd hired a long metal ramp to get Edwyn up the two front door steps. I had an additional wheelchair for the upper floor and various bathroom stuff. Amete and Hazel had the house looking squeaky clean and gorgeous. Fingers crossed.

I even had the car valeted, assuming we would go in it. Wrong again. Hospital insurance dictated that we go in a mini cab. Ours is not to reason why.

The home visit started with me meeting the occupational therapist and her student in the car park, where she showed me how to use the sliding board, a banana-shaped solid piece of plastic, to slide Edwyn, in about six stages, from the wheelchair and into the front seat. And there he was. Armed with sick bags we set off on the journey which would take about thirty or forty minutes. As we drew nearer to home I asked him if he recognised our local area?

No, nothing at all.

I pointed out landmarks, but still no recognition.

Near our street I wondered if he was excited? His answer: 'Trepidatious.'

Relating this to Pip later, she said that earlier that day Edwyn had described his feelings as 'apprehensive'. Impressive.

At the house we got him into the wheelchair. Hazel had already rolled out the ramp and through the front door he came, for the first time since he was carried out on that freezing February night. We pushed him straight through to the kitchen, where the first thing he saw was the large Tretchikoff print on the wall, a moving-in present from our friends Pav and Henri. Tretchikoff is the famous artist who did all those Woolworths pictures that hung above the fireplaces in a million working-class homes when I was growing up, including my own. Edwyn had used one, *Tina*, on the cover of 'A Girl Like You'. But the Pav and Henri picture was a less-often seen portrait of a 60s beatnik girl. And Edwyn recognised it instantly. And also made its connection to Pav.

Later he would tell me that he actually couldn't remember the house at all until he came inside. Then, to his immense relief, it dropped into place. And that had been the source of his apprehension.

We had a trial run with Edwyn on the stair lift. Success. Then he came back downstairs to our living room, to gaze around at the various bits of ephemera, all of which belonged to him, including Rudolph, the stuffed fallow deer head he's had since 1982, bought in Brick Lane when he first moved to London. Rudolph gets keys and tour passes hung on his antlers and when Will was a baby, he was his best pal. We'd sit him in his baby chair, dummy in mouth, in front of Rudolph and they would stare into each other's big eyes. Then there's the huge EMT turntable, bought cheaply from BBC redundant stores, which would have been used to spin discs at Radio One or Two before being replaced with computers. His stuffed heron, his stuffed kestrel, the other ones that I can never remember the names of. A lot of stuffed things. His boxes and boxes of charity shop singles. His James McIntosh Patrick watercolour, given to him by his mum, because Edwyn was friends with the painter when he was little and Mr McIntosh Patrick already an old man.

Edwyn kept pointing at things, registering recognition in great excitement.

The occupational therapists went off to measure the height of the bed and the toilet and do various other OT things and the three of us, Edwyn, Hazel and I, settled for a few minutes' peace with a cup of tea.

And then we did something unashamedly sentimental. Just before illness struck, Edwyn and Seb had completed the recording of his new album. Three of the tracks had even been mixed. Some weeks before, Seb had put them onto a CD for me and when I had finally talked myself into listening to them, late one night when I came home from hospital, it was nearly unbearable. I had ended up curled in a ball on the floor.

The first song, you see, was called 'Home Again'. When you listen to it, you can't help but think Edwyn must have had second sight. Now I asked him if he was ready to listen to himself sing for the first time. He agreed and we played 'Home Again'.

I'm home again
Hardly certain of my role and then
I started searching for my soul again
But there was nothing I could find
Unwhole again
But I've been here before, old friends
And I know I'll be consoled again
In the past I've left behind

When I was a boy
Well, I heard somebody singing
And I heard the guitars ringing
And it brought me home again
Home again

I've strayed again
My good intentions got mislaid, and then
I got stuck inside this maze that bends
Have I been this way before?
I've stalled again
Like some eternal drunken brawl that ends
When the mirror finally cracks, and then
There's no reflection any more

Outside on the street
Well, I heard somebody singing
And I heard the music ringing
From some clapped-out pirate station
It was my unholy salvation
Home again

It's killing, isn't it? He's brilliant, a wonderful songwriter. Floods of happy tears all round. Even the occupational therapists were affected, listening in as they sized up the bathroom.

For the return journey, I had a go at transferring Edwyn

into the car, successfully, so now we were free to travel independently, unsupervised. Fantastic.

A sublime day, full of the promise of better days to come.

•

A WEEK LATER, we had an all-important, inter-disciplinary, bring-the-family meeting in the day room. The end result of all the assessing. The most significant thing about this rather awkward, formal gathering was that we would be given actual projections for Edwyn's progress: targets that each therapy area believed could be achieved and a timescale for each. And, most significantly, a proposed discharge date.

First of all the doctor, a registrar, introduced herself and invited everyone else to do likewise. There were about twelve people in the room, including Edwyn, Hazel, Will and I. The professionals introduced themselves in turn, identifying their role, then our lot, finishing with Will, who announced: 'And I'm Jonathan Woodgate, professional footballer with Real Madrid.'

As a joke, it didn't really take with the assembled professionals, which made it even funnier to Hazel and me. I was in danger of being seized with an attack of schoolgirl giggles. Compose yourself, woman.

I still have the written notes of this meeting. After reviewing Edwyn's current situation, we received the electrifying news that they anticipated his departure to be the middle of August, by which time they hoped he would be walking. With assistance, not brilliantly, but walking. Could this be real? They seemed fairly confident. His senior physio would later warn me of her fears for the quality of Edwyn's walking in the future. His dense lack of sensation would always interfere with the ability to confidently bear weight and she cautioned that this could severely limit his capacity for walking. At this point, I didn't worry. All I could think of was walking of any description at all. To be up on his pins, and how it would change not just Edwyn's life, but mine too. I happily admit to these rather selfish thoughts.

My respect for the long-term wheelchair user, the self-dependent user, the more dependent and their families and carers, knows no bounds. It's hard negotiating this world of ours, designed with the young and fit in mind. It requires strategic planning and ingenuity, not to mention grit and stoicism. Our nightly jaunts were an assault course. First, foot rests of the wheelchair out the way and shoes and socks off (to avoid slipping), then to a standing position to get the track suit bottoms off (Edwyn wouldn't be seen dead in them in public), and then sit back down to get his jeans on. Stand up again to fasten them then back down again. Shoes and socks back on. Up again, jacket on. Back down. Foot rest back, pick up the sliding board, off we go. In the car park, brake on, foot rests and side panel off. Position the board, slide Edwyn, then place his foot, slide again, other foot in, sort him out, seatbelt on. Collapse the chair, sling everything in the boot, off we go. Get to Harrow, do the whole thing in reverse, bar the jeans. Perambulate around the town, have dinner, back to car, repeat the process. Back at the hospital, whole thing in reverse again. Up to the ward, undressing, teeth brushing, into bed. Various parts of the chair on and off again *ad nauseam*. At home, most of this every time he went on the stair lift. Each time we entered and exited the house I would haul the heavy metal ramp back and forth to the front door. And Edwyn was able to offer me some assistance with his body weight – that's not an option for some people. How lucky were we. Our five months of intensive wheelchair use gave me an insight into the lives of others I will never forget.

•

THEN, SOME MORE thrilling news – Edwyn was coming home on the weekend. Just for a few hours, on Saturday, to begin with, but the momentum was beginning to build up. You would imagine that Edwyn would be ecstatic at this news. I'm afraid not. Having seen his home and reconnected with it, he could see no reason why he should not be there, right now and for good. I reasoned with him that if he could only stay in hospital until they had fulfilled their commitment to getting him walking, it would be worth putting up with. Edwyn felt he could do it all from home. I wanted to take advantage of what the RRU had to offer. We were locked in daily conflict over this and it was increasingly hard to bear. Edwyn is so persistent, tenacious. He rather wanted it all and wanted it now. His daily mantra had become: 'Get me out of here.'

So, home we went for the day on Saturday morning. Officially, we were to spend four hours at home, no more. Why? Because 'they' say so. Honestly, they were so bossy it was ridiculous – I'd even been told which chairs he was allowed to sit on while he was there, the few which were deemed a suitable height. On no account was he to be allowed to have a lie-down on the couch, because it was too low and getting back up would involve a deviation from his prescribed standing-up routine. The occupational therapists were to organise the local social services team to fit a cage around the loo, put my lovely new sofas (bought just before Edwyn's illness) up on blocks and generally turn the house into a nursing home. My tongue was shortening by the day I was biting it so much. Still, I had the comfort of knowing that unless I harried and harassed, the chances of the local social services doing any of this vandalism were the same as me playing beach volleyball at the Olympic Games.

For me, it was wonderful to be driving along with Edwyn, just the two of us, heading for home. Just to be free of hospital supervision for a few hours, on our own turf, was a heady feeling. To be in the car with him in his old familiar position, the passenger seat (Edwyn has never learned to drive), was another affirmation of hope.

We arrived home to a hero's welcome. Andy (the honest guitar dealer) and his partner Susan were there. Since he had been given the all-clear on the visiting front, Andy had been the most stalwart support. As well as rallying the troops now that Edwyn could really appreciate a visitor, so that lots of his musician friends were coming to see him at Northwick Park, Andy had been supplying Edwyn with meat-based, hearty, delicious home-cooked meals on his regular hospital visits. Since Edwyn had tipped the scales at ten stone, back in the MRSA days in the Royal Free, he had put on a little weight, maybe half a stone, but was still very light for a man of his height. So Andy was a man on a mission to feed him up.

Nan was there for a short weekend, and Will, of course, and we were joined by Paul and Jeni Cook for a happy lunch, followed by a lie-down on the forbidden sofa by Edwyn, where he received his friends like a consumptive heroine from a Victorian novel. Then it was time to take him back, many hours after we'd been told to, crazy rebels that we were. (I did get a little ticking off, but I could take it; I was forty-seven.)

·

THE FOLLOWING WEEKEND we negotiated our first overnight stay on Saturday. The hospital was slightly reluctant about this, but as my good old sis the expert nurse was joining us yet again, I had extra leverage. We rolled out on Saturday morning with Edwyn's hospital kit piled on his lap. After a peaceful day at home, broken only by a bit of physio I'd been instructed on, and a visit from Andy and Susan – just doing normal things at home was such bliss – it was time for bed. Edwyn was a really early-to-bedder, about 9 pm, and would remain so for a long time. This first night and for a few months to come, he couldn't make it to our bedroom on the top floor as the stair lift didn't extend that far, but would sleep in the spare bedroom on the middle floor. He didn't want me in with him (an offer politely declined) and I tucked him in in his customary position, flat on his back. He still could not roll on to either side. I used to look at him and imagine it to be pretty uncomfortable, but Edwyn seemed accustomed to this unnatural state of repose. However, my bedroom felt a little too far away for me to leave him, so, ever the fusspot, I made a bed on the landing floor outside his door. During the night, just as I had with Will when he was a baby, I went to check on his breathing, to confirm that all was well. Considering how many nights I'd had to leave him to the tender mercies of hospital staff this was completely dotty behaviour. But I couldn't quite get over the sight of him sleeping in a bed in his own home. So he had to tolerate me poking him gently through the night, just to confirm that he really existed.

Sunday morning dawned and I was allowed to join him for a bit of a doze-in. I lay there almost managing to pretend that life was what it once was.

Andy came and made Sunday lunch (a mercy mission he has repeated dozens of times since) and after a great day, we hauled ourselves back to the hospital. Edwyn was infuriated. There was to be no reasoning with him from now on. I would remonstrate with him that he was spoiling our time at home by moaning about going back, but he had the bit between his teeth and would not budge.

'Hospital life is shit. Get me out. No. No. No. Help me, Grace. Get me out.'

I remember a miserable night when Paul joined us for dinner at Nandos (I didn't make him eat there *every* night; we had two or three other options we rotated) where Edwyn spent what could have been a nice night out badgering me incessantly. It was pissing down with rain, suiting the mood, and when we said goodbye Paul, with Edwyn's complaints still sounding in his ears, looked at me with such sympathy it was all I could do not to burst into tears. Andy also had to bear the brunt of an industrial amount of moaning on his visits and was enormously patient with Edwyn. He and Susan witnessed some of his more extreme outbursts of fury, some in public. None of us embarrass easily, fortunately. And as hard as Edwyn's frustrations were to deal with, they were entirely understandable and, in social-worker jargon, appropriate. I admired Edwyn's consistency, his energy, his determination to have his way. It was so in keeping with the man I had always known. If he had been any different, I would have found that much more worrying.

•

THE WEEKS ROLLED on. Gradually our home stays were extended until, for the last couple of weeks, I could pick Edwyn up after therapy on a Friday afternoon and his timetable would be so ordered that we didn't need to go back until Monday lunchtime. Still not good enough for him. Nothing but total freedom would suffice.

•

He took her hand
They took the floor
She was his all-time favourite dancer
Smiled lopsidedly

Decidedly
Awkward, he asked her
Take my hand
Take me and
I'll take my cue
Ain't you guessed by now
I dote on you?
The late bus is leaving
From the lonely station
So grab your silk stockings
And your dance invitation
~ Intuition Told Me (Part 1), 1979

Incredibly, I can't remember when Edwyn first walked. There wasn't a 'Eureka!' moment, just a gradual steadying, a little more balance, two people on either side, lots of standing practise and lots of work on his foot, which had 'dropped' – the tendons had shortened and Edwyn's heel would no longer strike the floor, something common in stroke and brain injury. This is a stubborn issue, requiring aggressive and consistent physio to produce improvement, often proving fruitless. On the RRU, most patients were splinted to deal with it and Edwyn was no exception. He had a temporary cast while he waited for the permanent, moulded plastic splint, called an AFO (an ankle foot orthosis), a most cumbersome contraption. You need one shoe a size bigger than the other to accommodate it. So you have to buy two pairs of everything.

But suddenly there he was, walking a few steps in the corridor, a physio and assistant on either side, holding a four-footed walking stick. Each day building up a few more steps. Then, walking with just one physio. I wasn't allowed to walk him for a while. Then I was deemed competent, but was warned to only walk with someone else on the other side. At home, this was not practical. We did it our way and I resorted to lying through my teeth again.

It was too hard, sticking to the rules of the RRU. A new guy had appeared on the unit, Chris, a twenty-two-year-old who, following a kicking from which he had barely escaped with his life, had been airlifted to the Royal Free for neurosurgery. He was coming back strongly, however. I had no doubt he would make a good recovery, but meantime, he challenged every inch of the RRU's authority. He was loud, he was sweary, he used to watch *Scarface* at top volume on his portable DVD player three times a day. (Another of the RRU's bizarre rulings banned these players. Chris defied them. After all what could they do? Wrench it from the grasp of a stroke patient?). He was accused of 'inappropriate' behaviour. I was intrigued. What had he done now? All in all, he was great fun, livened the place up, and Edwyn and I cheered him from the sidelines as he stuck his big, awkward thorn into the flesh of the regulations.

Edwyn's first steps in the outdoors happened one Sunday afternoon, in our local Queens Park, with Nan pushing his wheelchair gingerly behind at collapsing-back distance. We were jubilant. From now on we were firmly in the zone. Every day would bring some small gain. And homecoming was beckoning.

•

BY THE BEGINNING of August, practically everyone on the unit was beginning to get sick of Edwyn's complaining. As always, he was a willing and compliant therapy candidate, but a miserable soul the rest of the time and, eventually, Pip, who was his staunchest supporter, recommended him for early release. In truth, Edwyn and I were so fortunate, as we had it all going on, unlike the vast majority of the inmates of the RRU, for whom their stay would represent their best exposure to valuable therapy. We had options, where most did not. Edwyn looked to me to get it all sorted out, whatever he needed, and get him the hell out of there. Pip met us to give us the good news, with a few provisos. Edwyn could leave at the end of the week, but the hospital firmly recommended he come back as an out patient (most unusual) for a few more therapy sessions the following week, because he was on a bit of a roll in all departments.

Edwyn was also in the middle of a course of Botox treatments – not designed to make him look more like Cliff Richard – but injected into his right arm and the leg for the purposes of reducing spacticity. These were proving quite successful. In theory, although they relaxed the muscles, they ought to have knocked out any feeling, making any controlled movement impossible. I don't know why, but Edwyn got the relaxing benefit without the knock out. In fact, I thought I could get a little more responsiveness from these limbs when he was on the Botox. We would continue with it after he left hospital.

We were more than happy to agree with Pip's suggestions. She also told us that the department had discussed it and would like to extend to Edwyn an invitation to return to the unit for more in-patient therapy a few months down the line, when he might possibly feel a little more positive about spending time on the unit. I felt quite shamefaced about this generous offer, appreciating its value and the commitment of the RRU to Edwyn's recovery. Edwyn was warm and polite to Pip. He showed himself in his true colours, however, as soon as we were out of earshot: 'No way!'

Oh dear, what was to be done with such an ungrateful wretch?

•

I PACKED THE huge suitcase again for the last time, and trundled it to the car park, ready to transport Edwyn home. OK, we'd be back at the crack of sparrows on Monday for a 9 am appointment, but he'd spent his last night in hospital. I felt weak at the knees.

During all those months when I could see no end in sight, I would occasionally indulge myself in a fantasy of what coming home would feel like. Now that it was upon us, I wasn't disappointed. I swung between pure elation and a simple, warm contentedness. He would be with us again. Will would have his Dad back. Whatever this life would turn out to be like, we would make it normal life, our family life, as we would define it.

Fifteen years before, when we had had Will, we experienced a little bit of outside interference, as everyone does, from health visitors, midwives, that sort of thing. Far from seeing this as valuable support for us novices, Edwyn and I used to put a face on when they were around, then gratefully shut the door and decide to do everything our own way, as it suited the three of us. Having spent many months of experiencing life completely beyond our control, we could not wait to seize it back, to close the door on the professionals. The troubles ahead would belong to us, our responsibility, our solutions. No uninvited interference need be tolerated any more. Edwyn's mood had already altered. He looked very satisfied with himself when I glanced across at him, sitting smugly in the passenger seat of his own car, going to his own house, to sleep in his own bed.

By the time we arrived home, the anger and frustration he had been displaying for months had entirely evaporated. From now on, he would be almost always happy, positive, upbeat. All it took was coming home.

While we were driving along on that memorable afternoon, my mind crowded with scenes from the past and visions of the future and feeling a little overwhelmed, Edwyn, ever the pragmatist, had already begun to make plans. Staring straight ahead through the windscreen he announced firmly: 'Grace, read.'

BACK TO BASICS

THE REALISATION THAT reading was lost to Edwyn had come to me quite early on, before Trudi had arrived on the scene. Prior to his illness, Edwyn had been working in conjunction with a label called Domino on a very smart release of the earliest Orange Juice recordings called *The Glasgow School*, after the art movement of the same name. The record was due out in March 2005 and the label wondered if they could still go ahead? I immediately assented as I had no doubt Edwyn would want me to. I brought in a magazine with a long article covering the release, including the last interview with him before his haemorrhages, and showed it to him. His eyes scanned the words uncomprehendingly. He began turning the pages, quickly, unseeingly, clearly troubled. Nobody had prepared me for this and, crazily, in those early days I had never made the link between speech, reading and writing. So this was the moment I experienced the realisation that Edwyn, who loved Lermontov, Goncharov,

Zamyatin, Fitzgerald, Brautigan and Salinger, could no longer read. It came to me like a blow to the solar plexus. And I had to hide my shock because I could see the fear in his eyes. To reassure him, whilst desperately trying to mask my own reaction, I had said: 'A step at a time, Edwyn, we'll get it back.'

Almost six months later, he hadn't forgotten my promise.

'You want to learn to read again, Edwyn?'

'Yes, help me.'

'We'll have to start at the beginning, with children's books. You don't mind?'

'Not at all.'

The speech and language therapy he received in the rehab unit involved very little structured reading recovery, mainly because it is so time-consuming that nothing else would get done in the short periods allocated in the course of the week. We had done a little practise, using newspaper headlines and other pieces of bold print, but while he was in hospital it was hard for us to properly structure a reading recovery programme. Edwyn realised the time had come.

•

AND SO, FINALLY, he was home. We cracked a bottle of champagne with Andy, Susan and Nan. Afterwards, Edwyn had his usual early night, safe in the knowledge that this time there would be no return to the strange and horrible existence of hospital.

It must seem so ungrateful to be so desperately glad to be shot of both hospitals. They saved his life and got him walking again. But a very nice sister on the RRU summed it up. Asking her if they often got the chance to see what became of their patients further down the line, she answered, 'Sometimes, but not as often as you would think. For some of our patients, this place represents the worst time in their lives. They're not in a hurry to revisit those days. Understandably.'

Edwyn fell into this category of patient, for sure.

•

EDWYN'S FIRST SHOWER at home was interesting. Nan and I attacked the unfortunate man in a pincer movement as we attempted to give him his first proper experience of the newly fitted-out bathroom. Up until now, I'd gone for the easier option of a strip wash on our weekend visits home. The logistics of showering were not straightforward. Small room, awkward angles, two chairs, and transferring him up a step from the wheelchair to the special shower-ing chair. Nan and I wound up in hysterics, shouting ludi-crous instructions at each other, ('forward momentum!'), although I'm not sure Edwyn found our performance so hilarious. It was like having Laurel and Hardy give you a shower. But the first attempt is always the worst. By the first Sunday morning home, we had refined the technique and built in moves that one person could manage. Edwyn gains in confidence the more times a move is executed so that he assists too, making the whole process much less tortuous. So now he had the luxury of a daily shower in his own new bathroom. So different from the hospital facilities, which had given me the creeps.

Edwyn has called me a hotel snob, going all the way back to our touring days in the 1980s, when we could sometimes only afford the most basic places. I hated it. I recall guest houses where it was advisable not to put your bare feet anywhere on the floor. He never minded much, having done many 'nylon sheet' tours in the early Orange Juice days, but when we graduated up the scale I was very relieved. The nouveau riche in me does love a nice hotel, I admit. When Edwyn was away without me and we would talk on the phone I'd say, 'How's the hotel?'

'Well, not bad, but not exactly a Grace hotel.'

Or, 'Very much a Grace hotel.'

He has kept this mockery up for years. So, closeted together in the grotty bathrooms of the RRU, I'd mutter, 'Definitely not a Grace hotel ...'

•

BACK AT THE RRU, Edwyn had three days of therapy sessions to complete and another dose of Botox. On Wednesday, after lunch, when the unit was quiet, we slipped unceremoniously out of the back door. From now on we really were on our own. Edwyn had a final quote that I recorded in my diary.

'Help me, please, discover what I am.'

'Okey-dokey, Edwyn, I shall!'

•

IN THE COMING months and years there would be many times when the *hugeness* of what had happened to us would hit me with such force that I would be rooted to the spot. I would be daunted and scared at the thought of the future. I would yearn so much for things to go back to how they had been. The changes in Edwyn were, and still are, profound, and sometimes I would feel as if I were in mourning for his old self. Sometimes this would translate into behaviour that I'm ashamed of. I have often been short-tempered, impatient, nagging. But it would be Edwyn who would rescue me from the worst excesses of bad temper, from dark, despairing thoughts. Once free of hospital, his mood completely lifted and, although there would be moments of frustration and annoyance aplenty, he has never succumbed to despair or bitterness. His remarkable self-belief, initially only a glimmer, would soon grow to a bright flame, and would carry us both forward. That and the wonderful backing of family, friends and top-notch therapists.

The progress that Edwyn was set to make over the next few months would be so dramatic it led me to muse on the powerful force that home was exerting on his neurological functions. Maybe he had been right after all. Should I have brought him out of hospital earlier? Who knows. I was excited and grateful to see that he was lapping up what had quickly turned into a frenetically busy schedule like a man possessed. Our community occupational therapist (we had one for a while) was concerned that I was setting too strong a pace, but I was being led by Edwyn. The idea that he

could be made to do *anything* that he was not in accord
with was laughable. When he was tired, he told me so, and
we rested. But his drive, to my joy, was formidable.

•

PLANS FOR THE future were afoot. It was time to get the
sleeves rolled up.

We would now be reunited with Trudi. She would soon
be up-to-speed on the progress Edwyn had made with Pip,
and ready to make plans for the big push. (Note the royal
we. Every now and again Edwyn will say to me, when he
considers I'm unduly harsh or insensitive, 'I've had a stroke
you know!'

After the first few times I began to counter with, 'Yep,
and I had it right alongside you, dear.' This is unfair, but he
knows what I mean.)

I had also planned our next physio move. A practice
called Heads Up! (the exclamation mark is important)
appeared to be a solitary island of neurophysiotherapy, a
very particular specialty, in an otherwise vast desert of nothingness in the south east. Their nearest outpost was at Park-
side hospital in Wimbledon, a good hour and a half drive
from us. But that was fine. I had lined up an appointment
for a week later with the physio there, Ellen MacDonald.
This was to be a hugely significant meeting.

On a warm Friday in August, we drove across the
Thames to the hospital, which bordered Wimbledon
Common, to meet Ellen for the first time. I was laden with
all my RRU tackle, like a good student wishing to make the

right first impression. There were various arm splints, leg splints, shoulder slings, the quad stick, and even a piece of headgear – a slab of moulded white plastic with straps fastening under the chin which had been made to protect the space in Edwyn's head while he did his physiotherapy. Apparently he was submissive about this while he was in hospital, but I could never get him to agree to wear it with me. Point blank refusal. It offended his vanity.

We sailed in, Edwyn in the wheelchair and me carrying my enormous kit bag. Ellen sized us up while we took her in too. She was Australian, late twenties, slightly built but strong looking. She had a no-nonsense personality which took about two minutes to identify. She would later tell me that she had to hide a smile when she looked at us laden down. She had worked at the RRU for a while and recognised the signs. Her assessment of Edwyn's physicality began immediately. Shoes and socks off, shirt off so she could observe his entire torso (he always wore shorts for physio from here on), and out of the chair. Edwyn could walk, supported on one side by his quad stick and on the other by a person. From now on, as well as building up his tolerance, it would be all about the *quality* of his walking. Edwyn, quite naturally, was overcompensating on his left side for the things he could not do on the right. But it was important to combat this left-side leaning, which did all sorts of mad things to his upper body, to build confidence that he could use his right side, even if the feedback he was getting from every area there was minimal.

This would not happen overnight. The work was intensive, gruelling and repetitive, and the gains came slowly, with some spectacular exceptions. In consultation with Ellen, and in order that Edwyn would get maximum benefit, we agreed on three sessions a week. Apart from his resting arm splint, which he wore overnight to reduce spasticity in his hand and arm, Ellen was not keen on continuing use with the rest of the kit. Edwyn was given a normal walking stick. She also recommended a very clever gizmo that we use to this day, to help combat foot drop.

I believe it was on our third visit to see Ellen that we had a conversation about what goals Edwyn would like to aim for in the short term, his priorities. Edwyn, as he often did then when asked these questions, looked at me. I had no hesitation. Stairs. Just a few stairs, two even, would make all the difference in the world. We could get in the front door without the wheelchair and the ramp, and that would be a very big deal.

'You haven't tried stairs yet, Edwyn?' Ellen seemed slightly surprised. 'OK, let's do it.'

Before he could even think about it we were in the corridor and Edwyn was mounting a flight of stairs, holding on to the railing on the left, and leading with his left foot on each tread, while Ellen gently assisted the placement of the right foot. *A whole flight*, just like that. I stood open-mouthed. How was he going to get back down? Just the same as he got up, except that on the way down, the right foot was placed first and then the left followed, having taken the strain. Clever, clever. Ellen's expertise allowed Edwyn to follow her instructions with total trust. I was hopping up and down with glee. My next question came fast. How soon could we try this at home? Very soon. We'd give it a couple more sessions and then Ellen would give me the all-clear to have the stair lift taken out. I would need an additional rail installed, so we had one on either side, and some outside ones too, but goodness me, I hadn't dared hope to be rid of it this soon. I have never been so glad to have had poor value for money from a purchase! (In fact, the stair lift company take them back and even give you a bit of a refund.)

So this was the beginning of Edwyn's partnership with Ellen. As a working team, they suited each other perfectly. Neither suffered fools gladly, both were outspoken and both were hard workers. In Edwyn's case, almost all the time. He had his moments. I recall Ellen working hard on his foot one day, when Edwyn interrupted with a lengthy, disjointed soliloquy about how difficult it was for him, how deserving of understanding he was; really giving her the old sob story. She stood, holding his foot in the air, looking at him quizzically, eyebrow raised. When he was done she said, briskly, 'Finished? Right, back to this foot.'

Edwyn liked that. 'Ellen, you're awful. But I like you!'

Most of the time, he was putty in her hands.

•

SAD TO SAY, the same could not be said of his attitude to me. My notebooks are crammed full of exercises we were encouraged to follow through on at home. I was so anxious about progressing, about not sliding backwards, about getting it right. But Edwyn simply hated doing exercises with me. Attempts at gaining his co-operation on physical jerks was to cause more friction between us than any other single issue. The psychology just didn't work very well. Edwyn was extremely resistant to me telling him how to do things. I suspect that if I could see a replay of my coaching style I would hate me as well. I'm sure I said, 'You do want to get better, don't you?' a few times. I may have come over a teensy bit patronising occasionally, as well.

When we discussed the problem with Ellen he would simply say, 'Grace is terrible. Oh, terrible.'

If I'd ever tried to teach him to drive, which I hadn't, because he had no interest in learning, I suppose I would have realised how tricky it was going to be as his mobility coach. Even now, when I try to explain to him how much better off he would be by adopting a policy of blanket submission, accepting that I know best in all matters, he will have none of it. Strange.

•

BUT NO MATTER, Ellen was doing an extraordinary job, I did my best, and we pushed ahead. Towards the end of August, my friend Pav and the stair lift company dovetailed with another so that the lift could go and the rails could be installed, all on the same day. In the afternoon, when Pav had finished, he joined us in the back garden and asked if Edwyn wanted to try a climb. There are thirty-seven stairs from the ground floor to the top, where our bedroom is. Edwyn climbed them all, without a pause, three weeks after coming home from hospital. He could now place his right foot without assistance. For a while, I would follow behind, for safety. Slowly, with some adjustment, but independently. And then, at the summit, having had a tour around our bedroom and bathroom for the first time since February, he descended in one take. Now he could sleep in his real bed, beside me, whether he liked it or not.

•

AROUND THE SAME time, now early September, we left the wheelchair in the car park and walked the short distance to the physio block and into Ellen's treatment gym, without mishap. Then, one night soon after, we had dinner in a local restaurant on Kilburn High Road and decided to walk home. It was a walk of about a quarter of a mile. A virtual marathon. I promised Edwyn he could have as many rest stops as he needed. I knew there were a series of walls on the way that we could flop down on if need be. But he didn't stop to rest once. I was still holding his arm at this time, gently supporting him on the right side, but he was doing all the hard work. After that, I folded the wheelchair up and put it in the studio store room. We've not used it since. Even at airports we decline assistance, which would mean sitting in a chair. The staff look at me like I'm barking mad sometimes and Edwyn wavers a little at the thought of miles of corridors. But it's a good workout; we leave ourselves plenty of extra time and he gets stronger.

I have no phobia of wheelchairs or their users, quite the reverse. I have lost the hesitancy of the able-bodied around the wheelchair-user. I have a much better understanding now of what is involved. It's just that, having come so far, I can't bear to contemplate any step backwards. We must always be going forwards. What a tyrant I am.

●

DURING THIS MAGICAL first month at home there were to be two more red-letter days.

The first was Edwyn's forty-sixth birthday, on 23 August. What should we do? Edwyn was never one for a fuss about birthdays, but this was special. So, I booked a table at the Savoy Grill, in the art deco splendour of the Savoy Hotel, to enjoy Marcus Wareing's great food. We were a party of eight: Nan and Will, Andy and Susan, Pav and Henri, Edwyn and I. All of us beautifully suited and booted, we gathered in the American Bar to toast Edwyn. We toasted him several times that lovely evening. The food was gorgeous, the welcome was warm, the company perfect. Is it possible to have more to celebrate? I was blissfully happy, with my family, with my friends, with Edwyn. Writing now, I can conjure up the feeling, heart full. As we waited in the foyer for the taxis home, I saw Will having a right old chinwag with the commissionaire. As he helped us into the cabs, the gentleman complimented me on my son's lovely manners. That just about finished me. Back home, Edwyn couldn't believe he'd made it past midnight without flagging.

The second great event was Edwyn's first tentative return to his studio. This had not been possible until he could climb stairs, as the studio is a level above ground, above what would once have been the stables for the fire station's horses, and are now garages and lock-ups. My mother confided in me that during the hospital days it occurred to her that the logistics of simply getting through the door of the studio were immense. Could it be done? Yes, it could and here we were, tackling it. The steps up to the first level are a little tricky, being of cast iron construction, a type of fire escape, really, with gaps between, which were somewhat disconcerting for Edwyn. We had several capable fellows in attendance however. I can see Pav now, confidently placing Edwyn's foot in a firm and safe spot on each tread, as he climbed the stairs, surrounded by bodies happy to cushion the blow should he wobble. Which of course he didn't.

His entrance to the studio was somewhat muted. This is a complex and confusing world of which he was once lord. More than anywhere in the world, this was his home, an environment packed with detail that demanded encyclopaedic knowledge from anyone who would master it. Edwyn no longer possessed that knowledge. As he wandered around, looking at things, touching things, Seb pointed bits out, reminding him of when he acquired this, what he used to say about that, their favoured methods of using the lovely vintage microphones, little anecdotes from their recording past. But it became evident that we were in information-overload territory. You can't have everything, all at once. I picked up from Edwyn a feeling of recognition and love of his studio, but also a patient acceptance that there was a great deal more work to be done before he would be ready to return.

Seb and Edwyn would make an attempt at working on the mixes of the album which had been recorded the previous year, but Edwyn was not able to contribute much and decided to shelve it for a while. Seb did rough mixes of the whole thing for Edwyn to listen to, to mull over. He even suggested that he could try and finish the thing on his own, without Edwyn. It absolutely cracked Seb up when he got a response in the negative: 'That would be an ... aberration!'

I had not heard these tracks yet. Edwyn and Seb seemed to have magicked this record out of nowhere. I had been in my office during the days of its recording, but largely stayed out of the way. Most of the work had happened at night time. They were past masters at what they did and required no interference from me or Hazel, or the 'office girls', as Seb archly referred to us. He used to leave us notes on the desk from the night before: 'Office girls, need ink for the printer.'

'Office girls, so and so phoned, re such and such. Get back to him. Now please.'

'Office girls, blah blah not happy about quote. THIS WILL NOT DO!'

Since Edwyn had fallen ill the funny studio rhythm the four of us had shared for years had fallen apart. While he was in hospital, I would have occasion to go up there, where for many months it was dormant, quiet as a tomb. I would wander around, seeing Edwyn in everything, all his glorious confusion. It would make me heartsick; I felt bereft, broken, and would scurry away, back to hospital, back to the urgency of here and now. For Seb it was a rotten

2001 © Rankin

time. The studio without Edwyn, with all the uncertainty of the future and all the echoes of the past. Very hard.

Edwyn may not have been ready to go the whole hog in the studio yet, but he could visit it. The place was alive again. Seb and Bernard Butler, another friend, musician and producer, were keeping the home fires burning. Edwyn's studio had a reputation of its own and it has continued to grow even as the boss has been wending his winding path back to fitness. In fact, Duffy's world storming debut album, *Rockferry* was largely recorded there, with Bernard producing and Seb engineering.

•

AS AUTUMN LENGTHENED and winter approached, we made the long journey three times a week to Wimbledon for physio. The intensity of these treks I can still conjure up. Hours and hours in the car. We passed the time in conversation. I would talk, gossip, rant and rave and, initially, Edwyn would mostly patiently listen. In the early days of hospital I was issued with some leaflets advising me on the best ways of communicating with a person with aphasia. Here is some of the generally held advice:

- Allow plenty of time.
- Leave lots of space.
- Give clear messages – one idea at a time.
- Be flexible. Try different ways to get ideas understood.
- Use straightforward language.

- Don't shout.
- Check understanding.
- Don't anticipate what the other person is trying to say.
- Don't make assumptions.
- Eliminate background noise.

I agree with all of the above. I just wasn't brilliant at sticking to it. In stark contrast to the guidelines:

- I would have the radio on, join in with the debates (talk over the top of them) and prod Edwyn to get involved.
- I only know one way to talk. Non-stop.
- I think I probably bombarded Edwyn with ideas.
- I did check for understanding and obligingly said the same thing many different ways (infuriating for the listener).
- I continued to use flowery and complicated language. Edwyn's usage of the English language had never been simple, but he had the advantage over me of succinctness.
- I was always anticipating what he was trying to say. We'd often reach his point through a lengthy process of elimination.
- We ate out a lot, often with friends, in noisy restaurants, buzzing with babble. Edwyn struggled to separate conversation, to follow threads. I was very aware of his predicament, but the company meant a

lot to him and, with practise, he did get much better at coping over time. These days he has no trouble whatsoever in holding his own.

So, as sound as the guidelines are, Edwyn had to tolerate my approach which, although I initially worried that if I couldn't undergo some sort of personality transplant he was going to be hampered in his recovery, turned out to suit us. Trudi (and after her, Sally, Edwyn's other speech therapist) would very kindly not castigate me for my shortcomings, and they saw plenty evidence of them. Before long Edwyn would resort to ejecting me from his speech and language sessions as soon as he realised I was entering the prattle zone.

•

WE USED TO try all sorts of exercises in the car. I had a little book written in the 60s by an amateur therapist called Valerie Eaton Griffith, called *A Stroke in the Family*. She had devised a series of exercises, written and spoken, which had helped the actress Patricia Neal, first wife of Roald Dahl, come back from a near fatal haemorrhage which had left her severely aphasic. I adapted some of these for our purposes. For instance, I would ask Edwyn to list me six David Bowie albums. By October/November he would do well on this kind of question, which he would have found much harder in earlier months. Or synonyms and antonyms (harder). One thing that worked very well was when I began a sentence and left Edwyn to finish it, often with hysterical results. So I would say, for instance: 'Whilst crossing Wandsworth Bridge the other day I couldn't help noticing that ...(Edwyn) ... life is strange and beautiful!' The answers were always mad, random and gleeful.

We did a lot of reading practice as we went along. Edwyn was a compulsive reader of street furniture, advertising, van logos. As he attempted to read every sign we passed it made me realise how little conscious attention I pay to the ridiculous amount of signage our city is crowded with. There is one that says 'Controlled Zone'. They are *everywhere*.

•

EDWYN'S TECHNIQUES FOR speech recovery and reading recovery were necessarily repetitive and could come across to the unwary as dotty behaviour. I knew better, even from the start. It had to be done as his own form of brain training and he had no interest in the impression he gave others. His natural ego has been his saviour in this regard. Sometimes he and I are given a nice pat on the back for helping to 'raise awareness'. In truth, Edwyn is detached from thoughts of how much or how little the world at large understands his experience. It never crosses his mind. He is entirely absorbed by his own life, his own fight. The impression formed by others is simply none of his affair. I take great delight in my role as onlooker as Edwyn engages with society at large in his own unique style. Mostly people are great, especially as Edwyn confronts the issue head on, announcing to taxi drivers, waiters, all strangers who register on his radar: 'I had a stroke, you see. Six months in hospital. Not good, but I'm doing well at the moment. I'm getting there. I'm enjoying life.'

At this, most people open up, discuss someone they know who had a stroke, compliment him on his tenacity.

Occasionally, there is an awkward moment. Arriving in Glasgow recently, the plane touched down and the usual flurry to get off ensued. I was helping Edwyn on with his coat when an impatient guy behind shoved into him.

'Excuse me,' said Edwyn.

'No, you can excuse me! I was here first!' retorts Mr Impatient.

I explained that Edwyn had had a stroke and needed a bit of help, hence my squeezing in.

'Well, that's just brilliant …'

Eh? I'm sure it was awkwardness that made him say it.

Edwyn turned to him, wagged his finger and declaimed in a loud voice: 'Just you behave!'

The poor guy couldn't wait to get off. I was, of course, doubled up.

•

EDWYN APPEARED TO have developed a mellow, tolerant side since his stroke, much to my disgust. On our trips to Wimbledon, as well as badger Edwyn to get into current affairs, or whatever the hot topic *du jour* happened to be – weighty or flighty – we listened to music too. Radio 2 was often on. We got into frequent disputes about the quality of the music. I found it mostly unbearable. He was much more complimentary.

'Edwyn Collins, a nice guy? I'm not having it.'

'Yes, I'm sweet and lovely now.'

Back in the day, he was known for his vitriol, sideswiping his contemporaries, playing with journalists, alienating all and sundry in interviews, a real smart mouth. I used to despair of him and celebrate him in equal measure.

Foreign journalists were a particular target, especially European ones who specialised in the banal.

Asked for the umpteenth time why he had called his band Orange Juice, he would say: 'Because there was already a group from Scotland called Middle of the Road.'

Puzzled silence.

Or, to a Dutch journalist: 'Because, in my country, Scotland, we have a drink called orange juice.'

'We have that drink in Holland too.'

'Do you?'

See what I mean?

Now he was pleasantly indulging all sorts of nonsense. I decided he was doing it to annoy me. There was a particular song on the radio that winter, 'Nine Million Bicycles in Beijing', which Edwyn claimed to love. It made me scream. An old music business lag called Mike Batt co-wrote and produced it.

'Here we are at Wimbledon Common, Edwyn. If you can correctly identify the connection between this record and Wimbledon Common, you win a big frothy Starbucks.'

'The Wombles!'

'Correct' (Mike Batt had his first hits as a singer/songwriter with 'The Wombles' in the 70s).

We listened often to Seb's rough mixes of the album. I will always associate this record with those car journeys. I watched Edwyn deep in contemplation, as if he was trying to introduce himself to his former being, the man who had conjured up this layered world of ideas, words and instruments. *Was that really me?* was written all over his face.

'I used to be an intellectual.'

'I'm daft now.'

'I need to get better. I must get better. I will get better.'

•

Revolution on the south bank
I poured poison in the think tank
Got out before the big crash
I caught the tail end of the whiplash
Staying out of the spotlight
Don't get blinded by the limelight
I'm going back to the backroom
I'm operating in a vacuum
~ Back to the Back Room, 2002

THE OTHER MAIN thrust of recovery rested, of course, with Trudi. Her thrice-weekly sessions with Edwyn took place in the comfort of our living room, at the dining room table, which was soon groaning under the weight of books, notebooks, sheaves of speech-therapy materials, Scrabble tiles (used to help him reconstruct words from their component letters) and pencils. Trudi's strategy covered so many angles, was so varied, so fascinating. Understanding the true nature of Edwyn's language loss and the multifarious means of encouraging its retrieval took a long time for me to wrap my brain around, never mind Edwyn.

When I quote Edwyn in this book, I'm showing him off at his finest. Particularly in the first year following his home-coming, speaking was a task involving enormous effort and concentration. Trudi worked on his word production, his sentence construction, his cognitive understanding of linguistics and his reading and writing. Writing techniques were much more difficult to produce than reading, which Edwyn and I could beaver away on at our leisure, having been furnished with the correct strategies by Trudi.

Edwyn was tested on nouns and verbs, repeating the tests with a gap of a few months in between. The tests were done by video. A set of objects was shown, about seventy, and then footage of people or things involved in actions, or reactions. So, nouns and verbs. I was possibly cheating a little when we did it the first time, because I wanted to encourage him. I would pause the video to give him a little more time as the images passed by quite quickly. His score on naming the nouns, about thirty-odd out of seventy, was much better than the verbs, about fifteen. Edwyn likes to be able to quantify his improvement wherever possible, likes to compare where he is now to where he was then, so tests like this are great, because each time we repeated them the score would have increased as well as the speed with which he was able to complete the test. It also underlined what we already knew, that work on verbs was an area to concentrate on, to make speech more fluid, more understandable than trying to deliver his point as a list of nouns, his favoured method. For instance, he would say:

'The man? Oh, sixties man. Hmm. Dundee, yes? New York. Oh, the guitar. The man. No, help me.'

He might be talking about Lou Reed; he might be talking about anybody. The Dundee reference might be when he remembers first seeing him. He needed an immense amount of support to convey his meaning. But fortunately Trudi had seemingly limitless ideas in her armoury and slowly, he advanced.

•

ON THE WRITING front, Edwyn's problems were deep and complicated. I worried that he would never again be able to generate independent writing, the difficulties were so extreme. When we write as literate adults we employ a number of complex skills. In Edwyn these had been obliterated. We begin with the letter and the sound it makes. He couldn't picture the letter A if you said it to him. To give an idea of the magnitude of the task:

The letter A. What does that look like?
No idea.
If you asked him to write a simple word like cat:
C-A-T.
Nothing.

Breaking it down to its component sounds. Cuh, ahh, tuh.

Still nothing.

Asked to separate out the first sound of that word from the others, once again a blank was drawn.

Writing about it now, I am amazed to remember Edwyn's commitment, his acceptance, his patience, his will to work, and above all, his courage. We assembled a list of key words for each letter of the alphabet, chosen by Edwyn. I seem to recall putting a lot of it together on one of our car journeys. He uses this keyword system still to help him visualise letters. It is easier to do this in the context of a real word. A is apple, F is fish, H is hotel, U is utopia. He uses lots of familiar names in the list: David, Myra, Grace, Nan, Petra, Edwyn, William, Robert. For a long time this work was more or less agonising, with tangible results coming so slowly. If a short sentence took you twenty minutes, with help, you could be forgiven for thinking that useful, independent writing was beyond your grasp, and therefore, lead you to question the point in the gigantic and exhausting effort to achieve such little reward. But Edwyn ploughed on.

EDWYN HAD BEEN working hard to find his way around a computer again. In order to achieve this he would have to re-acquire some tricky moves, things that we take for granted. Principally among them:

Sequencing: Making each move in the right order. From opening the lid of the laptop, switching on, choosing which application to open and so forth. Initially he needed to be cued up for every move.

Scanning: Casting his eyes around every area of the screen to find the area he should move the cursor to next. It was very easy to miss things. He had blind spots.

Selection: Sifting through the options presented on the screen and making a choice. Which requires self-confidence.

Typing: Edwyn had to familiarise himself with the keyboard lay-out as if he had never seen one before. He also had to train his left hand to type and navigate the mouse pad. Taking his on-going battle with dypraxia into account, this was no mean feat.

In fact Edwyn was making terrific progress, perhaps because we could lead him to sites that really interested him. He had been an avid eBay buyer, one of the first in this country to cotton on to it, and was quickly able to recall his username and password. An automatic function, often repeated, which returned with ease. Amazing. I was also fascinated to see that his understanding of numbers had not deserted him. He was not so hot at verbalising numbers, but when he saw the prices that vintage guitars and microphones were going at, for instance, he was fully cognisant of what he was looking at. He would shake his head and say sadly, 'All my bargains have gone away.'

I tried him on sums, too. To my astonishment, although oral calculation was unsuccessful, written work was pretty hot. I made them harder, with old-fashioned multiplication sums and long division. Still very good. Not always perfect, but pretty impressive.

•

BACK ON THE eBay trail, I asked him, 'Do you want to bid, Edwyn?'

'These prices? Pfff ...' His sharp eye for the going rate was working perfectly.

Eventually, he did have a go. And, with him making the decisions on how to pitch for it, he won a very peculiar-looking old guitar from the 1920s which, he explained to me, would have been a real cheapo back then. It has a strange chequered print on it and is just exactly the type of oddity that would have caught his eye in the old days. A few months later I opened my email to find that he'd pressed ahead with a bid on an amp, all on his own, no help. Another milestone had been reached.

'Crazy, I suppose. I can't play.'

•

To anyone who's followed me
I offer my apology
I'm splitting up
I can't afford to compromise

231

With someone I don't recognise
I'm splitting up
The idea first occurred to me
While shaving rather cautiously
Because I bleed easily
My head is separating from my heart
I'm splitting up
~ I'm Splitting Up, 2002

FOR MOST OF his first year out of hospital, Edwyn, on pondering his career in the light of all that had happened, would say: 'Retired, I think. A good innings. How many albums? It's a lot, I suppose.'

He would deliver this assessment a little wistfully, a bit sadly, but with a sort of resignation.

Andy, Seb and I would always respond the same way. Let's just wait a while and we'll see.

At that time, Edwyn couldn't see a way back to song writing, not least because he could no longer play the guitar. Edwyn's right hand and arm have continued to be most stubbornly unreceptive to therapy. We keep them both in good order, with not too much tightness, but useful function seemed a big ask. Prior to his illness, I would have assumed that the loss of his ability to play the guitar, something Edwyn has done every day since he first picked one up, would have been too crushing a blow, really unbearable. And yet, he lives with it. It makes him sad, it makes us all sad, but it has to be accepted. And, with resourcefulness, worked around.

'You are and will always be a guitar player, Edwyn. Nothing can remove that from you. And a collector. Carry on.'

In fact, Edwyn and I had been playing the guitar together, after a fashion (I'd had to take a crash course, never having played before), for a few months. In Northwick Park, Edwyn had several sessions with a guy called Matthew who worked for Nordoff-Robbins Music Therapy. This organisation is the music business' favourite charity, with an annual awards ceremony as its major fundraiser. Edwyn had been involved with the Scottish wing since its inception. We couldn't have imagined that he would end up as a recipient. I only saw him with Matthew twice. The first time I walked in on the end of one their sessions I was confronted with the astonishing sight of Edwyn playing the guitar and singing. Well, both of them doing it together. Edwyn's left hand making the chord shapes, as it always does in a right hander, and Matthew strumming. The left-hand bit is obviously the more complicated thing. And singing together, a Beatles song, Edwyn lagging a little behind, the words suddenly unfamiliar. But what a thing to behold. Obviously, I would have to learn to strum: Edwyn knows dozens of guitar players but none of them are on tap, as I was. Strumming isn't as easy as it looks, if you're a woman in her late forties who has, until this moment, never shown any hint of ability or inclination to play. The instructions would be rapped out: 'Slow down!' or 'Speed up!', but with a little practice, I was soon strumming upwards as well as downwards. I quite fancied myself. And with Edwyn doing the clever stuff, I could almost convince myself I was playing the guitar.

Sadly, I haven't progressed very much. It's a pretty basic approach. But this seems to suit Edwyn. One of the first things he did was to work out chords for his hospital epic, 'Searching For the Truth'. And then he came up with a nifty little middle eight (for those that don't know a middle eight is the bit of a song, usually in the middle, that introduces a bit of added interest by breaking up or moving away from the simple structure. It tends to be eight bars in length, hence the name). All with me strumming along good style.

Will picked up a guitar for the very first time, just shy of his seventeenth birthday, and hasn't put it down since. Carwyn Ellis, our friend and Edwyn's band mate, who can play literally anything brilliantly, took him under his wing and showed him his first chords when Will started to show an interest. Until then, we were not sure he would go this route. He used to look at us when he was younger and say: 'Don't expect me to go into the family business.'

We never did, and Edwyn was very adamant about not pushing him. He has a clear belief that if you are going to be a musician, you will be. I'm not sure this applies in the classical field, where teaching and discipline are so important, but certainly in the confines of rock and roll, I agree. Edwyn is self-taught and so is his son. Edwyn came to it at a similar age and was similarly obsessive. I'm sure Will would have started playing music regardless of his dad's illness, but there is a special joy in watching him play, now that Edwyn can't. His father offers advice and corrections, which they sometimes argue about, as I look on with a beatific, motherly expression. Although I am *slightly* put-out about my role as chief strummer being usurped.

·

WILL WAS ALSO fantastic in helping in his dad's recovery in another way. He introduced Edwyn to something that would prove to be the most valuable weapon in our armoury as we fought on with the battle to recover writing. MySpace. To the uninitiated, it's one of those dreaded social networking websites. But to Edwyn, it was to be the key that unlocked his creative writing abilities and helped him tentatively back to the domain of the written word. This site works particularly well for bands and musicians as you are able to use it as a shop window for your music, old and new. You can also keep those who are interested abreast of your activities and receive feedback from your 'friends'. Being a bit backward and out of touch, we had never heard of it when Will introduced us to the idea. Within minutes of creating his profile, however, Edwyn was receiving online correspondence. This really excited him: instant feedback from the outside world, a world he had felt so cut off from since his illness. I had shown him the huge quantity of messages he received while in hospital and explained how they had helped sustain me. He had really appreciated them, but MySpace feedback was current, about where he was now. It also had things he could count. Post-stroke, Edwyn likes counting, a lot, as I mentioned. He still appreciates quantifiable things and MySpace gave him plenty of measurable data.

I also introduced him to the world of blogging. In my

own world, I'm not keen on all this self-absorption stuff, but I could certainly see its potential for Edwyn. We began working on his mail, postings and blogs together, every day. Edwyn would mostly dictate, but would also try a few painstaking words on the keyboard himself. I would add a little dash of artistic licence, to tidy things up, and all in all it worked rather well. As we went along, he gradually tried more and more words. We assembled a book of his most frequently used words, favourite catchphrases, odds and ends, which we still add to today. It took more than a year of undiluted MySpace addiction but, two and a half years after his stroke, he was answering his own mail, unaided. His letters are short and sweet, but the progression continues at a steady pace. This is a mind-boggling miracle to me as I was deep inside Edwyn's aphasia for a long time. I knew what the intricacies of it were, so to see him with this degree of independent ability restored to him was breathtaking. And wonderful. But I don't underestimate the achievement. Nothing walks to him. He fights tooth and claw for each victory. Press on, Edwyn.

•

YOU WILL REMEMBER Edwyn's instruction to me as we left hospital for good to get going on reading again? We were slogging away at that, too.

Our niece, Sarah, was five. Hazel, her mum, still had some Ladybird Key Word scheme books that she had started Sarah on. Hesitantly, she suggested them to me, not sure how this would go down.

Perfect.

Edwyn couldn't have cared less about the simplicity. The task had begun and that was all that mattered.

I bought all the other books in the Ladybird set, which divides learning into twelve stages, three books in each. They have become unfashionable as a tool for early learners in schools, which amazes me, because they work. The idea is simplicity itself. Most of us will remember them as the 'Peter and Jane' books. The books were launched in the 60s and were written by an educationalist called William Murray. He used to work as an adviser to a borstal and went on to be the head of a school for what was then called the 'educationally subnormal' (ah, those halcyon pre-PC days!). When I tell Edwyn this he pipes up,

'That's me!'

Murray's research, together with an educational psychologist called McNally, found that 100 words make up half of everything we read, speak and write, and a further 300 words account for three-quarters of our verbal input and output, and thus they devised the reading scheme. The beauty of this system for Edwyn, once again, was that progress was clearly demonstrable as you move up the levels of difficulty. We could look at where we were and place it in the context of where we had been last week, last month and, eventually, last year. Edwyn would never be quite sure he was getting better at anything unless you could show him concrete proof.

Although the Ladybird scheme was designed for children in the first stages of reading, Edwyn was learning to read again in quite a different way to a child. As time went on, it was clear that he retained a memory of what it meant to be a reader and of the content and meaning of many of the books he had read in his life.

I recall during a session with Trudi he had dug out some of his favourite books and she was using them as the basis for a discussion. Trudi's skill was such that Edwyn would become immersed in thought and unexpectedly produce a full sentence, heavy with relevance and lyricism. One book, *Oblomov*, by a Russian called Goncharov, almost defies description its themes are so abstract. But Edwyn found his way to the core of the thing:

'A man brought to the brink of disaster by his man-servant.'

And Trudi helped him write it down. Can you imagine the pure elation I felt as I saw this indication of potential revealed?

Often, but not always, he could recognise complex words immediately, on the front page of a newspaper, for example. Words like 'policy' or 'referendum' could suddenly jump out at him. Words which were descriptive, or loaded with meaning, like 'angry' or 'turquoise' also seemed quite recognisable. But the most-used words – like *this, them, those, there, then, where, when, were, was, with, up, on, of, in, if, is, as, at, are* – all of these were pure Greek. The most stubborn of all were, incredibly, *a* and *the*. He would stare and stare at these two. There is so little to them, that they would give him no clue as to their identity. Thousands of times I would have to step in and say them, before they

started to stick. He also needed very large print to work
with. Hence he could cope with headlines in newspapers,
with help, but not smaller text. The effort required to
restore a reasonable degree of familiarity with the little
words, the 'abstract' words with little integral meaning, was
immense. Every day, building it up, grinding it out. It could
be deeply frustrating and tediously dull. It could also be
wonderful, satisfying, pleasurable. You never really knew
how it would go from session to session. We both had to
dig deep to keep going with it some days. And in the
context of all the other therapeutic activity going on, the
temptation to skip a day was great. But we almost never did.

I can't quite remember how long it took us to get to the
end of the scheme. Several months, anyway. We moved on
to proper books with stories for kids. And within much less
than a year, to a series of books I found to be really brilliant.
An Edinburgh publisher called Barrington Stoke produces
books that have been specifically adapted for young people,
including teenagers, with reading difficulties like dyslexia.
Books with older themes but printed on a cream-tinted
paper which has been proven to be easier to read from. Also
the typeface has been researched; the spacing, the font size.
These proved to be an enormous boon. I was introduced
to them by an independent bookseller in Wimbledon,
after I had described our predicament. As Edwyn slowly
progressed through the months, again I could select from an
ascending level of difficulty, to keep nudging him forward.
No sooner would he have mastered a stage than I would
annoyingly be shoving him on to the next. Infuriating for

him, as he often would have preferred to luxuriate at a nice comfortable level for longer. Lots of deep sighing and tutting would accompany each new beginning.

I'm not a natural teacher. My patience, not my strongest suit, would soon be exhausted if Edwyn proved the least bit resistant. Whilst we made great progress and most sessions were quiet and satisfying, reading together was not always a peaceful activity. We could get on each other's nerves and, unforgivably on my part, would from time to time get into a fight. Edwyn would get fed up with the effort and clam up and I would start lecturing and hectoring. Then I would hear myself, stop dead in my tracks, overcome with guilt, beg his forgiveness and promise never to get like that again. Until the next time …

•

WE LIVED OUT the last months of 2005 in a kind of a dream. Life was so busy, lots of appointments, tons of therapy, but there was soon a pleasant rhythm established and the novelty of simply being home from hospital had certainly not worn off. We were a little blissed out. Among all the hard work there seemed to be plenty of time for just enjoying life; a heightened appreciation of the pleasures of spending time with each other and Will, with family and friends. Edwyn had lots of visitors, everyone joining in a reserved celebration of his homecoming and returning strength. Every day we would go walking, the quiet winter months being the best time in London's parks and heaths. It felt like we had them to ourselves. Gradually increasing our distances, at first Edwyn walked with his stick in his left hand, me uncurling his right hand and supporting him on his weak side. Then he no longer needed me as a prop and he could go further without needing a rest. To walk a circuit of Queen's Park without stopping was a goal we aimed for. By mid November he achieved it.

•

IN PHYSIO, ELLEN had prompted Edwyn to try walking without his stick at all and had been impressed by his bravery at trying this. She explained how scary it is when you have such limited sensation on one side of the body. Like stepping off a cliff. Edwyn trusted Ellen implicitly and would try anything if she said he should. So we then would try a few steps without the stick during our walks. Although effortful, he soon increased his range. By springtime we had increased the circuit to take in the top half of the park, more hilly terrain and he would do a goodly part of it with no stick. I walked along slowly beside him often feeling the cold, whilst Edwyn would be boiling hot with the aerobic effort.

We had many crisp, winter walks on Saturday afternoons in beautiful Regents Park, bundled up in duffel coat, hats, gloves and scarves, usually followed by an early dinner at one of our favourite spots in Marylebone High Street.

Edwyn had forgotten London, his home town for over twenty years. He didn't recognise Kilburn, or Queen's Park, or any routes as we criss-crossed the city on our way to appointments. I kept up a running commentary, pointing out landmarks, recalling stories and incidents from down the years to give him some context with which to jog his memory. Over time this bore fruit and as we walked the streets and parks, the clouds would sometimes suddenly part and Edwyn would exclaim, 'Oh, oh, I remember! It's back!' How exciting for him. How incredible these moments of illumination must have been.

.

IN OCTOBER, WE were having Sunday lunch at home with Susan and Andy, who, once again, had cooked, when Edwyn froze in pain at the table. I was terribly alarmed. The pain was in his leg, something new. After about a minute of squawking, the pain was gone as quickly as it had come. Edwyn started moving his leg around in wonderment. He had instantly acquired a few degrees more feeling. Moreover, the low level pins and needles that he claimed to have had constantly for months had completely gone, never to return. We looked on speechless as he stomped up and down shaking his head in disbelief. Ellen had no explanation for it. It's the mysterious thing that is brain recovery. It will sometimes defy explanation.

.

'REAL' LIFE, OF course, would still intrude on the routine, from time to time. We were at the hospital one morning for another nine o'clock Botox appointment when the house had an attempted break-in. This was actually the second time in a year. We were burgled while Edwyn was in Northwick Park. I came home from hospital one night, around ten, walked in to my living room and took in the broken glass, half brick on the floor, missing laptop, iPod and camera. A narrow side window had been smashed, so the culprit must have been very slight, most likely a youngster. My alarm had been on the blink and, of course, I hadn't got around to dealing with it. I sat on the floor, looked around and decided I couldn't care less. Compared to what we'd been through and were still in the middle of, it seemed like so much nothingness to me. Will was at Hazel's that night and came back over with her; sister to the rescue as usual. Hazel fumed as the police didn't bother to show up until the next day, when they got a piece of her mind. They sent round a right pair of thickos.

> Cop: 'Where did they come in then?'
> Hazel: 'The broken window? Obviously it's a kid, the size of the opening.' (It's about six inches wide.)
> Cop: 'You'd be surprised. I could probably get through there.' (He's a big fat guy.)
> Hazel (note of derision): 'Go on then.'

I got the window fixed, put some bars up, got the alarm sorted – with a police monitor on it this time – and went about my business, putting the whole thing out of my head with ease.

Our prolonged absences from home had clearly not gone without being noted by the toerag element in our neighbourhood, though. As we returned from our Botox appointment I saw Amete and a police car at the house and our front door completely splintered. A passer-by had seen two young men kicking the door down; no mean feat as it was double locked. The person had witnessed one of them brace himself on Edwyn's handrails so he could kick it really hard from behind. By the time they had bashed through it, the alarm was activated, the passer-by had called the police and there was no time left to get anything, so the front door damage was all that was achieved. In the year that followed we were to have two further attempts, both fruitless. I can't say that it didn't bother me at all, the inconvenience of the damage, but I had a different perspective on minor domestic incidents of this nature. Water off a duck's back. I beefed up the security a little more each time as were obviously being targeted and forgot all about it. Touch wood, the last few years have been trouble free.

•

AT THE END of November 2005, Edwyn got the word that his titanium plate was ready and he went back to the Royal Free for his last operation. It was good news. The last bit would be done and dusted in time for Christmas. The vulnerable concave hole in the side of his temple, which we had become strangely accustomed to but which did look rather peculiar, would finally be covered. But, returning to the scene of my nightmares was unexpectedly hard.

In and around that building, I couldn't walk anywhere without flashbacks. Edwyn was relatively unperturbed about facing up to an operation, something which a year ago would have had him horrified. He had been through so much, he was inured to normal fears associated with surgery. We arrived on Thursday night, met the consultant who reassured us that they intended to give Edwyn a big dose of anti-MRSA drugs during the op, just in case, and that he wouldn't be in for any length of time. He met a few of his old nurses, including Jo, who had seen him through the darkest days. The unpleasantness of being in hospital again was offset a little by the pleasure of showing him off. I had to leave him alone in hospital overnight, but this time he was stronger, more able, and the comparison with the man who had been here earlier in the year was stark.

I was back at the crack of sparrows and Edwyn was whisked away. The operation was quite lengthy and I was allowed to sit with him in the recovery ward, something that had never happened before. By evening he was settled peacefully but woozily and I wended my way homeward, experienced enough to know that by the next day he would seem so much better. A quiet Saturday, with a visit from Andy with his trusty food parcel, and we were told that after a doctor's visit on Sunday, I could take Edwyn home.

We were back home by Sunday lunchtime. A couple of hours later, Edwyn shot a temperature, and butterflies took flight in my tummy. But the hospital reassured me that it was normal post-op behaviour. We held fast and soon all was well. For ten days Edwyn sported a long arc of steel staples on his shaved head, but this time the wound healed, no infection took hold. We were in the safety of our own home, far away from the bugs that stalk hospitals.

SCOTLAND

I'll take a train
I'll take a plane
Away up north where they know my name
But they don't bug me
The way that some folks do
I'll take this guitar
I'll maybe start anew
Because otherwise I'll stay down here and stew
Upon a Hill of Many Stanes
Five miles south of the Great Grey Cairns
I felt the full force
Of five thousand years
And I felt the sting of time's eternal tears
~ Libertccnage Rag, 2004

WHEN EDWYN HAD first recovered consciousness way back on intensive care in March, I had begun whispering to him about getting him better and about where we would go. To Helmsdale. I wanted to give him something to fix on, to aim for, and there was nothing that would have more meaning for him than this place.

Helmsdale is a small fishing village on the far north-east coast of Sutherland, which, along with Caithness, is the most northerly county on the Scottish mainland. Edwyn's mother's family go back generations in the village. It grew up in the early part of the nineteenth century when the inhabitants of the nearby strath (a wide river valley) of Kildonan were forcibly removed from their smallholdings by their landlord, the Duke of Sutherland, and either emigrated to the New World in vast numbers along with other evictees from various parts of the north of Scotland, or formed new fishing communities along the coast. This period is infamous in Scottish history, known as the High-land Clearances. Edwyn and William's ancestors became stonemasons and builders of some renown, rather than fishermen, and many of the buildings in the local area were constructed by them.

When we were first together Edwyn told me many stories of this magical place where he had spent every summer holiday of his childhood since he was seven, in the company of his grandparents. His grandfather, Dr Hugh Stewart Mackintosh, was born in the house in 1903, the middle child of a family of seven. A very clever and able boy, he went to the University of Glasgow at the age of sixteen to study mathematics. The education he received in the village school was first-rate. Some of his and his sister's text books on English literature and philosophy are still in the house, with handwritten notes in the margins, and attest to the high standard of scholarship it was possible to achieve in a small Highland school in the early part of the last century. Way beyond anything our children learn today. Eventually he became the Director of Education for Glasgow, a famous educationalist with an international reputation. And he was capped many times for Scotland as a rugby player in the 20s and 30s. Something of an over-achiever!

When I met him in his early eighties, he was still an impressive and slightly intimidating figure. He divided his time in his retirement between his home in Glasgow with Edwyn's grandmother and the home of his boyhood, now under his custodianship.

•

In 1985, I visited Helmsdale for the first time with Edwyn. We spent two weeks in September with his grandfather at Bay View, the family home. As we drove north, Edwyn recalled the thrill of driving to Sutherland with his Grannie (just as in our family, she was the driver: Edwyn's grandfather drove very little), as she marked off the rivers they crossed with an old song: 'The Dee, the Don, the Deveron...'

I don't know what I was expecting but after a few days marching the hills and the rugged coastline, for anything up to twelve miles a day, I started to think I was on a Duke of Edinburgh Award scheme rather than a holiday. I'm from the industrial central belt, and at twenty-seven had barely been exposed to proper outdoors conditions. As I looked up and ahead at the eighty-two-year-old man scaling a cliff or the steep face of a burn he would turn around and call to me, 'Are you all right there, lass?'

I decided to ignore the townie inadequate I was and press on, trying to keep up with Dr Mackintosh forged in steel, and Edwyn, natural mountain goat. The glorious surroundings, breathtaking, endless, empty except for the wildlife, distracted me from my screaming muscles.

'You're doing well, lass, you're not a moaner.'

'I'm doing quite a lot of inner-moaning, believe me!'

After two weeks, I was broken in, no longer felt the pain, transformed by the place. Coming back to the old house, cooking dinner and sitting by the fire listening to Edwyn and his grandfather re-shaping their relationship with one another as adults, I fell in love with every aspect of life in Helmsdale...

Edwyn had been so close to his grandparents growing up, but as he chose his unusual career path, I think his grandpa found the life he was pursuing and the music he made quite unfathomable. A man with a tremendous work ethic, ('Work, work, work, we must work, boy ...') the life of a pop star was entirely baffling. Walking along one of the many beautiful beaches with him one day, watching Edwyn in the distance exploring rock pools just as he had always done as a wee lad, Dr Mackintosh had a go at reaching for Edwyn's world.

2006

'I've been looking into this pop music. Now, would I be correct in thinking that the gist of the thing is, one takes a refrain and repeats *ad nauseam*?'

'That more or less sums it up...' I nodded in laughing agreement.

His Grannie, Mary Wilson Mackintosh, on the other hand, was fully accepting of Edwyn's artistic bent. As his number-one fan, she had his vinyl albums displayed around the house. The staff in her favourite Glasgow record shop would greet her: 'Here comes Edwyn's Grannie!'

When Petra and Myra put the memory book together for Edwyn back in hospital, there were many letters in it that revealed so much of the wonderful affection he was held in by his grandparents, for whom he was the first grandchild. As Edwyn grew up they exerted a powerful influence on him. When Edwyn was approaching his second birthday, his mother had an illness that confined her to hospital in Edinburgh and he went to stay with his grand-parents in Glasgow. Understanding the pain of separation, Dr Mackintosh wrote often to his daughter and she has the letters to this day. They were reproduced in big print for Edwyn in the memory book. A few excerpts serve to give an idea of this fascinating couple and their relationship with their grandson:

15 May 1961
Of course, we are all longing to have him – the trouble is going to be to keep him from being thoroughly spoiled.

He is such a fine wee chap. I'll get him into gardening with me. There are plenty of tools to satisfy his every wish, and ground and grass to scamper about on. At the weekends I'll take him personally in hand and introduce him to the things that mean so much to me.

28 May 1961

I've just come from a 'walkie' with Edwyn in Newlands Park. We always have great fun together on these expeditions ... and his tongue is never idle .... Before tea we had a game of football on the grass in front of the house – you could hear him laughing and spluttering houses away. And then in to tea. His appetite is good but his tastes are erratic. The banana was discarded halfway through and then he was on to pancakes and butter and jam. When he has had enough he says a decisive 'Feenish!' and slides off the chair.

15 June 1961

Edwyn was in glorious form – I don't think I ever saw him in such a devastating mood ... There was no stopping him and I can't tell you when I enjoyed myself more. It was particularly refreshing after the kind of day I had at the official opening ... it was good, especially good, to be with Edwyn, his eyes bright, his cheeks like apples and behaving like a variety star. We'll have to watch that we don't spoil him – and that's not going to be easy, let me tell you.

Later, when the children holidayed at Helmsdale letters flew back and forth. Edwyn had a mania for wildlife and by the age of ten was an expert on British birds and all sorts of other flora and fauna, much to his grandfather's pleasure.

5 May 1974
Dear Edwyn and Petra
Today is Sunday, a day of supposed rest here, so I've laid down my tools and wandered off along the shore to the Green Table, the Ord [beautiful local landmarks] *and beyond. What a wonderful day it has been. The sun was shining, the sea, green, flecked with white, and the wind was coming in at the headlands, clean and salty and aseptic. The tide was far out so I crossed over the Green Table into the Baden, past the Pidgeon's Cove and round Aulten-tuder burn into what we used to call the Breckan Face. Everywhere there were sea birds swooping over my head as they rose from their nests. I saw a few with 3 eggs, quite a few with 2, more with one – the rest – late developers perhaps – with none at all. Edwyn would have loved it – Petra too I'm sure. The cliff face was covered in celandine, sea pinks, blue-bells and hosts of yellow primroses. A wonderful display, and everything so clean and fresh. I felt the years lift off my shoulders and I followed the familiar routes of my boyhood days – and, wonderful to tell, managed them … I have yet to go to the Clett (Edwyn knows this favourite spot of mine) and there everything I saw can*

be seen in concentrated form. But I miss the guillemots and puffins that I used to see as a boy – perhaps the fulmars that I now see everywhere have pushed them out. But the razorbills are a delight, so immaculately dressed in their black and white and their stripes. Just like busy young advocates in Parliament House.

I have reproduced this letter in full because Dr Mackintosh describes so much more eloquently than I ever could the utter magic of an expedition day from Helmsdale and why Edwyn, and latterly I, are so devoted to the place. The route he describes is now familiar to me, but pretty hard work. I have never been to the Clett, a vertiginous cliff. Much too scary for me to try, but Edwyn has some hairy stories of his treks there. The birdlife on offer enticed him.

10 August 1975 (Dr Mackintosh to Myra)
On Friday we climbed over the Green Table into the Baden and, as the tide was well out, we managed to get round to the mouth of the Aulten-tuder burn and even further. I never went further as a boy than they [Edwyn and Petra] *managed to do. And they did it cheerfully and in great excitement. They are great on these outings: they'll climb anything and everything and quick to see and hear anything of interest. Very good companions – I could ask for none better. Plenty fooling too – the nonsense these two can keep up, mimicking some characters of their vivid imaginings*

255

in domestic scenes has to be heard to be believed. They carried on this dialogue all the way from far up Kilphedir burn till we reached Bay View. And they finished up fit and still full of cheer.

There are many more letters in the book, which gave me a glimpse of the intense happiness Edwyn felt when he was a child in Helmsdale. It was strange for Edwyn, aged forty-five and fighting his way back to health, to muse on the relationships of his young life. As he grew up into an awkward and headstrong teenager, who did fine but did not excel academically, relations were not always so easy in this tight-knit family, but affection and loyalty remained firm.

I love this next letter. When I read it to Edwyn in hospital, he was hugely amused and rather touched. The effort made to stretch across the generation gap is palpable.

14 September 1980 (Dr Mackintosh to Petra)
I think of you a lot, Edwyn also. I do hope that this sudden and most welcome publicity that he and 'Orange Juice' has got is not something that has happened more or less accidentally, and that it presages growing success and achievement. While I say that, it is comforting to know that he is doing something that he really enjoys, and even if his group were never to achieve major success, the fact that he is so compellingly involved in these interests of his is a guarantee that unemployment can never be the blight it is for so many young people. Good luck to the lad.

And the only letter surviving from Edwyn himself to his Grannie.

> (Undated, some time in the early 80s.)
> *Dear Grannie*
> *Sorry for being so negligent and* <u>*Lazy*</u> *with regards to*
> *your much appreciated letters. I hope you enjoyed us*
> *on T.V. I'm in the best of health, spirits, etc so don't*
> *worry on that score. The group's quite successful so that*
> *means a lot of arduous trips back and fourth* [his
> spelling] *to London. However, it sure beats 'working.'*
> *Ha ha. Love Edwyn. XX*

Edwyn and his Grannie's relationship was characterised by mutual mischief. She only died in 2007, at the tremendous age of ninety-seven. She was much affected by the news of his stroke: 'But he's so young.' She would refer to him as 'a darling boy'. Edwyn sang 'Home Again' for her at her funeral, which I'm sure she would have loved.

●

THE HOUSE ITSELF, Bay View, is part of the draw to Suther-land and Caithness. Built and extended by the various generations of the family, it is solid and cosy. In 1989, Dr Mackintosh died, a huge loss to his family. He was eighty-six, but because of the enormous physical and personal strength he exuded, it still felt as though he had died prematurely. The house passed to Edwyn's uncle and, nine years later, in 1998, he decided to sell it. For us, the timing was good. We were flush with the success of 'A Girl Like You', and to our great excitement, the place that felt more like home to Edwyn than anywhere else, was set to become ours. With much less occupancy since Dr Mackintosh's death, the house was in a rundown condition. It needed a lot of work. Edwyn doesn't like change and was worried that it would lose the old feel. He even used to talk about particular smells he associated with the place and how could we preserve them? I didn't really have an answer to that one. But all electrics, plumbing, roofing, walls, windows, floors, kitchen, bathroom decorating had to be tackled. The house had never had central heating. I thought that would be a good idea. Edwyn looked unsure; freezing at night was part of the Bay View experience. Thankfully, I won.

Two and a half years later (planning consents and Highland builders move very slowly … beautiful work, but slow. My brother David, an electrician and great all-rounder, had been a great help in the process) the house was finished and we spent our first summer there, getting it shipshape. It got the seal of approval from Edwyn. I hadn't ruined it. Much of the old furniture remained, the same feeling, but with a few more modern comforts. Even the smells came back eventually, apparently. I'm still not quite sure what they are.

I sorted out all the construction stuff and Edwyn did the pretty, homemaking bits at the end. Our usual reversal of the traditional roles (Edwyn has always claimed I have enough testosterone for both of us).

Since then we spend as much time as work will allow in Helmsdale. For me, that is never enough, but I look forward to seeing my dotage out in this wonderful house, in this wonderful part of the world. We have many friends in the community who have welcomed me. Edwyn is considered one of their own.

•

OVER THE HOSPITAL months we talked about Helmsdale many times. It seemed like a far-off dream. The idea of getting back there; longed for but hard to imagine.

The last time we were there was just a few weeks before Edwyn fell ill. He had been asked to deliver the address to the haggis at the annual Burns Supper, celebrating the birthday of Scottish poet and hero, Robert Burns, in the nearby hamlet of Portgower. This was a real honour to be asked to do and we had a great night. The Fraser family – Elizabeth, Donny, Ann and Lucy – to whom Edwyn is related through his great grandfather, had made him a memory book of that night and of other places and things in Helmsdale.

In late January 2005, our friends in the village, Tommy and Sharon, were just about to move into our house for a period of some months while major works were taking place at their house. We'd suggested they come and take refuge in Bay View, which is where they were living when they heard the news of Edwyn's collapse. They kept vigil there for us throughout those rotten months.

After Edwyn's successful operation to insert the titanium plate, we decided to plan for Christmas in Helmsdale. In mid December we did the traditional huge load-up of the car. Will put the discs for the journey in the CD player, including his annual Christmas compilation; he makes a copy for all branches of the family, and it's always a creative treat. Finally I piled Edwyn in the front and Will in the back (when he gets settled down for the drive in the back seat, with stuff piled around him, Christmas has officially started) and we set off.

We usually go north for Christmas; for many years we went to Glasgow and more recently sometimes to Helmsdale. For William, a Christmas spent in London isn't really Christmas as he likes to be surrounded by family and chaos. This year though, we were having a quiet one in the calm of Bay View. First of all we would spend a few days in Glasgow to break Edwyn's first really long journey and see the family on both sides. I didn't know how he would handle such long periods in the car, but you never will know until you try, I reasoned. Edwyn sailed through the journey with no difficulty. All we had to do was stretch the legs a little more often than usual.

We had a happy reunion in Glasgow and then the lovely drive northward beckoned. After all the horror, it was the sweetest relief to pull up at the house, to be welcomed by our friends who had made dinner, had the fire roaring. Utterly spoilt and utterly happy. The sensation of falling asleep with my family safe around me, back in the bosom of the Scottish Highlands, Christmas coming, was gorgeous.

•

AFTER A STROKE, walking on any surface that is not even and solid can be a bit of a nightmare. Edwyn was nervous of grass, gravel, uneven pavements, slopes, kerbs, the lot. But with a little gentle cajoling, he tried everything. And, like the rest of us, he's not keen on bad weather. We can do cold, sharp weather, but wind or rain are a pain. Especially together. *Especially* wind, which throws him off balance and makes him slightly panicky. He hates it.

Our biggest challenge to date was coming up. I was desperate to see him walk on a beach again. Under the old radiator in the kitchen his hiking boots had been standing guard, untouched, waiting for him to return. Sharon said she used to look at them first thing every morning while they were living at the house, a sort of talisman for her during the very scary days. They're old boots that used to belong to Edwyn's grandfather, inherited after his death. Later, she became so superstitious about them, nobody was allowed to touch them. She would clean around them. They had to stay exactly on the same spot. A couple of days after our arrival I called her to say sorry, the boots had been moved. I had got them on Edwyn's feet and we had hit the beach. The boots, with their high sides, gave him great ankle support on the squashy sand. Sharon and Tommy were jubilant. The boot vigil was over, all was well.

•

WE ARE ABSOLUTELY spoiled for choice when it comes
to beaches in the north east. Don't tell anyone, but the
weather is often beautiful and benign and we have a
plethora of wide, white sand beaches that go on for miles.
The access to some of our favourites near the house was
tricky and strenuous, so for our first attempt we tried
Dornoch. This is the county town of Sutherland, a hand-
some burgh, with its own small cathedral, an extremely
famous golf course and a magnificent beach that is easy to
get down to. On the soft sand, Edwyn found it more stabil-
ising to lean on my arm on the left side, rather than his
stick, so I could absorb his wobbles. This is a technique we
use on difficult ground to this day, so I now have an over-
developed, muscular right forearm. But a few steps on the
sand later, Edwyn protesting loudly, me whooping with
delight, Will trying to pretend he didn't know us, and we
had opened up another avenue to returning pleasures.

Nowadays Edwyn protests far less about a lengthy walk
on the beach, except when I make him walk into the teeth
of a winter gale. He's learned to be very suspicious of the
positive spin I put on the weather, the length of the walk,
etc: 'Just round that corner and we're there. Nearly.'

'Oh, look, there's the sun trying to come out.'

'How brilliant was that? Think how satisfied you'll be
we did that when we get back home. You were fantastic.'

'Look at the roses in your cheeks!'

I've been warned off using 'child' psychology by him

many times but I persevere. I use a variety of tactics. Bully-ing, wheedling, huffing, threatening, bribery, cheerleading. Sometimes all at the same time. As long as we get the right result, which is, Edwyn accedes to my demands. He wants to really. If he didn't want to co-operate, no amount of trickery would persuade him.

•

WE HAD A perfect Christmas. Nan drove up from Glasgow on Christmas Eve. On Christmas morning everyone was a little spoiled. We had the most impressive Christmas tree, acquired by Sandy, our friend and Bay View's head grounds-man and chief custodian when we're absent, from what he calls his 'private forest'. Between him and Tommy, nothing happens around the place but they know about it. In recent years there have been potential landslides, floods, boiler explosions and seized-up heating problems, all averted by the vigilance of our crack team. I cooked the dinner which, if I do say so myself, wasn't half bad for me, and we were joined by Tommy and Sharon. Over the holidays we had the chance to catch up with all the friends in the village, who gave Edwyn a warm welcome back. We saw the New Year in with David and Ricky and settled down for a few days' peace before heading south and back to the old therapy routine.

As well as our daily walks if the weather was being kind, Edwyn toiled an hour or so a day at the kitchen table on the holiday homework that Trudi had prepared for us. Another required element of his day was his drawing session. For this he needed no encouragement. He couldn't wait for all else to be done with so he could get down to drawing.

•

THE SON OF parents who were both artists (who met at art school), whose father taught drawing and painting at art school in Dundee, Duncan of Jordanstone, (renowned for its association with many of Scotland's most acknowleged painters of the twentieth century) for many years, and who grew up surrounded by painters who were friends of the family, it is perhaps no great surprise that Edwyn turned out from an early age to have a talent for drawing.

When he was nineteen and had dropped out of art college, he got a job, a real job, with a salary, for about a year, as an illustrator for Glasgow Parks Department. This job involved devising nature trails through areas of parkland, aimed mainly at schoolchildren, and then designing and illustrating the leaflets to guide them through, drawing the various flora and fauna they could expect to see along the way. Myra has preserved some examples of his work which have been reproduced in his scrapbook. They are meticulous, accomplished pieces of work. For a nature-loving draftsman this was the perfect job. Pretty jammy for a nineteen year old, too, I think. Sometimes he would guide parties of youngsters through one of the walks. These were often kids from the less salubrious bits of Glasgow. He tells how, on account of his unusual style, and his youth, the kids would shout at him, 'Haw sir, are you a punk?' (this is 1978/79). 'Yes children,' he would say, 'I'm Nature Punk …'

The parks department ran something called 'The Nature Trailer' as an educational aid, which Edwyn would be called upon to man. It was an ordinary caravan fitted out with various natural history bits and piece; lots of stuffed things. Edwyn recalls the young female resident taxidermist working away doing revolting things to dead creatures in her corner of the office. In the office! She wasn't too popular with other members of staff due to the smelliness of the job. Edwyn, of course, found it fascinating. One day the nature trailer was parked in a notorious bit of Glasgow called Bridgeton, where he came under siege as the caravan was stoned by the appreciative local youth.

When he gave up this, his only ever *actual* job, to throw all his energies into the band and the label, he continued to draw, contributing to the look and design of Postcard Records and producing his own artwork for record sleeves on many occasions down the years.

He used to talk of a fanciful project for his later years when being a pop musician would no longer be on the cards; he thought he would do a complete set of new illustrations of the birds of Great Britain. A big project, it would take years, but would be something to get his teeth into in his rock and roll decline, which Edwyn thought must surely kick in by the time you reached forty. (How times have changed; today the world is full of creaky old rockers, not so much growing old gracefully as scarily.)

He talked of wildlife illustrators from the past that he admired: Archibald Thorburn, Audubon in America, and Edward Lear, whose cartoonist flights of fancy he loved too.

When I sat by his bed, silently numbering his lost accomplishments, I wondered what, if anything, it was possible to do about drawing. I provided him with materials while he was incarcerated in hospital, but he showed little or no interest at that time. Shortly before he left Northwick Park, he began to draw a cartoon man, possibly a self-portrait. A natural right-hander, he had to try with his left hand. When he came home, drawing this figure became part of his daily routine. I called him 'The Guy'. I have about sixty versions of him. When I dug them out to show Edwyn, much later on, his laughing reaction was: 'I'm mad, totally mad! Why? Oh dear!'

But I happily watched him slave away over The Guy for a few months. Something told me he was helping Edwyn's brain to restore order, bringing certain things back into sharper focus. Like reciting lists of rock bands back in the Royal Free, repetition continued to be an important tool in memory retrieval.

One day, in late 2005, I gently suggested he set him aside and try a bird. Edwyn has an old *AA Book of British Birds* and from that he chose a wigeon. Then a teal. And a wren. A Canada goose. On and on – one, sometimes two a day. Each drawing named and dated. Edwyn consistently describes his early efforts as 'crude'. He was not only trying to relearn the skill, but teach his alien left hand to do what only the right hand had been able to do. But the form and line are evident from the start and it was encouraging and thrilling to see how fast progress came. Inside, his talent for drawing was intact, and he knew it. This was the first of his lost gifts to return and it represented a great deal to Edwyn. It still does; he draws almost every day, unless events interrupt him. When we return home from a busy day and I want to flop out for an hour in front of some mindless TV, Edwyn invariably makes a beeline for his seat at the drawing table. It never represents hard work to him, even if it does require concentration. The standard he draws to now is quite breathtaking. No allowances for the right to left transfer need be made, although, ever the self-critic, he still sees himself as a long-term work in progress.

Drawing gave Edwyn hope, self-confidence, self-belief. In November 2008, he held his first ever exhibition, entitled 'British Birdlife' at the Smithfield Gallery in London. Here is something he dictated as an introduction to the exhibition, with a little help in extrapolation from me. But these are his own words:

Ornithology (birds) has fascinated me for a long time. I can't remember when I didn't love birds. When I was a boy, I could identify every British bird, most of them on the wing. I collected stuffed birds, too.

I think I was eight or nine when I found a fledgling greenfinch in the garden in Dundee. My neighbour called it Tweety Pie. A female. I kept it in a shoebox in my bedroom. It would tweet from 5am onwards, but I was too lazy to get up until about six or seven. I found a bird man, an expert, who told me to feed it with special food called Swoop. You mixed it with water. I fed it from my finger and she gobbled it up. Then I helped her to fly using the back of the Lloyd Loom chair and tempting her to me with the Swoop. When she flew off she would sometimes come back in to visit if I left the window open. And later she came back to have her first brood in the holly bush. A charming tale!

Drawing has been always been part of me, a passion. My mother and father are both artists. They met at Edinburgh Art School and my father went on to teach at art school. So I suppose I was surrounded by it growing up. When we formed the Postcard label in 1989 to put out Orange Juice Records, I would illustrate a lot of stuff for it, although we had another brilliant illustrator, Krysca. And as my music career went on, I've always drawn and designed.

I thought I would do a collection of bird illustrations when I retired from music. I loved Archibald Thorburn, a Victorian illustrator, particularly. I thought it would probably take about ten years, a nice little project.

I had a stroke, a brain haemorrhage, in 2005. I couldn't say anything at all at first and I couldn't read or write. I couldn't walk to begin with. My right hand didn't work. I'm right handed. So, no more guitar. The first time I held a pencil, I could produce a scribble, and that was it. I was in a confused state. Where do I start? I had to learn patience.

Gradually I took my pencil more and more. At first I drew 'The Guy' over and over again. It's mad, totally mad! I have fifty drawings of him. He looks a bit like me. I can't think why I did it now. Maybe I was stuck, but I think maybe he helped me.

Then I drew my first bird, a wigeon. It's quite crude, but I was pleased with the result. Each day I drew at least one bird. I was tired back then, but my stamina has grown.

I could see my progress with each bird. Up, up, up. It's encouraging.

Until recently I only liked to use very cheap notebook paper. I'm a creature of habit. But I'm now using posher cartridge paper. It changes your style.

When I draw there is no interference. Since my stroke I am interfered with quite a lot. And this is not to my taste, although I have been very co-operative. But when I draw, I am in charge and I don't have a therapist or a wife bossing me about. I'm left to my own devices and in a world of my own. Drawing was the first skill to come back to me, so it meant the world. If I can draw, what else can I do?

My recovery began with my first bird drawing. And now I'm showing my drawings in an exhibition. I'm looking forward to seeing them like this. At the moment they sit in piles on my table. I'm back on board. The possibilities are endless!

Not only has Edwyn's drawing ability come back to him, but his appetite for it is greater than it ever was. The challenge of learning to draw with his 'unnatural' hand seems to have fired his imagination. How amazing that as he struggled to overcome the limitations his illness imposed on so many areas of life, he had the enormous boost from knowing that this one thing was at least coming back, better and better each day. Improvement, and the potential for

more of it, is where it's at for Edwyn, and drawing gives
him that satisfaction in spades.

•

SATURDAY 7 JANUARY 2006 arrived to burst our bubble
somewhat. We were still in Helmsdale. At the end of an
uneventful morning, Edwyn was drawing at the kitchen
table. We had just finished an hour or so's writing practice,
quite a successful session. I was a few yards away, folding
laundry. He uttered a short sound, of protest I thought, as I
accidentally bumped the table. Then again. As I looked up,
I saw him arch backwards stiffly, his eyes half-close and
his whole body begin shaking violently. I rushed towards
him, gathering him up, restraining him, reassuring him.
I knew right away what it was: a fit, a seizure. This had been
mentioned as a risk back in hospital but I had assumed,
wrongly it would turn out, that at this distance of time,
almost a year, the danger had passed. I called Will, urgently.
He usually needs me to shout several times before he pays
any heed, but I only needed to call twice. I hurriedly called
out Sharon and Tommy's number to him and, in spite of his
alarm, he did everything I asked of him perfectly: call our
friends, ask them to ring for an ambulance, explain that Dad
is having a seizure. I couldn't let Edwyn go in case he hurt
himself, he was still bucking in my arms. I wanted Sharon or
Tommy to talk to the emergency services; it would be easier
for them to give clear directions. Soon after, the phone rang.
It was the ambulance controller, looking to give me some
instructions. By this time Edwyn had stopped fitting but was

271

completely unconscious and breathing very hard. Tommy and Sharon arrived seconds later and helped me get him to the floor and into a more comfortable position. His hard breathing subsided. He gradually opened his eyes. Very disorientated, he was unable to speak or understand us.

The thoughts fly fast, the adrenalin races, the fear takes hold again. We couldn't go back, please, please.

From the local hospital it was a twenty-minute dash for the ambulance. By the time they arrived Edwyn was more conscious and we lifted him onto his chair. The world was swimming into focus again. He smiled and tried to co-operate. He was able to walk into the ambulance with me. Tommy and Sharon follwed on with Will in the car. Ever practical, one of them brought our car, so we could all get back. In the back, the paramedic asked Edwyn some questions which he answered firmly, checking himself as he spoke: yes, I know this, I'm OK. His name, his date of birth, a few other things. I could see the relief I felt mirrored in his face.

At the local hospital, the Lawson in Golspie (where John Lennon was taken care of after his road accident in the Highlands, incidentally), Edwyn was desperate for the loo. When he emerged, we saw Will looking urgently for him. He spotted his Dad, on his feet, smiling.

'Hiya son, I'm fine.' Anxious to put him at ease, these were the signs we wanted to see. Normal reactions, speech, concern for his boy. Phew.

We saw an incredibly kind duty doctor, who was absolutely lovely to us. He explained the implications and suggested that Edwyn needed to be referred now to a neurologist. He offered him an overnight stay, which Edwyn graciously declined. Should another seizure occur, in the short term, he suggesed an admission to the regional hospital in Inverness for assessment, otherwise we must wend our way southwards and sort out a referral via our doctor in London. Chances of a repeat? No idea, nobody can say. Maybe soon. Maybe never.

•

OVER ONE OF Tommy's homemade curries that evening, the shockwaves evaporated and Edwyn and I resolved to simply press on, deal with it and try not to worry.

A few days later we said goodbye to Helmsdale; on the one hand reluctantly, but knowing that we had issues to address, so, keen to get back to London, hopefully unscathed.

On the Glasgow stopover, however, Edwyn displayed the first signs that he hasn't quite got off scot-free. He was as worried as I was about the implications of repeat seizures on his recovery, and began to display the symptoms of heightened anxiety. I knew the signs well. Until Edwyn's illness, panic attacks were something I knew about but hadn't been able to empathise with. In the last year, I had been introduced to this unpleasant side effect of shock, having had my own experience of delayed reaction. Not at all nice to see Edwyn go through it.

THE MUSIC

WITHOUT MEANING TO, and probably as a result of inner stresses I wasn't admitting to, I was about to put Edwyn in some potential danger. We had arrived back in London on Saturday evening, a week after our northern drama. We were both a little exhausted and enjoyed a lie-in on Sunday. In the afternoon I started to fret inwardly that Edwyn hadn't done much walking practise recently and persuaded him into his boots, which we had brought back with us, and off for a short hike on Hampstead Heath. The circuit I planned was one I was familiar with and was quite short. It needed to be. We got to the heath shortly before four o'clock. In January, there is not much daylight left at this time of day. A twenty-minute stroll would do, then repair to the pub for a warm-up.

I don't know how on earth I managed it, but I got us lost. Then I thought I knew where I'd gone wrong and got us even more lost. Before I knew it, we were hopelessly lost, in the encroaching darkness, in the middle of Hampstead Heath. We walked a fair way, towards some twinkling lights of houses, without passing a soul. Visions of helicopter rescues started flashing through my deranged mind. Outwardly, all was calm, as I did the 'nearly there!' thing for all I was worth. Edwyn was beginning to worry: 'I'm struggling!' At one point we even doubled back along a bit of bog land. Thank God for Grandpa's boots.

I had my phone with me, but it had only the tiniest little bit of battery power left. I used it to do what I always do in a crisis. Phone a sister! I got Hazel, thank God. I told her I was aiming for the nearest point at which I could get us off the heath, but had no idea where that would be. She jumped in the car and started heading in the general direction. I switched the phone off to conserve the power. From out of the gloom a nice young couple emerged on their way off the heath. They stifled their incredulity at the sight of me supporting Edwyn on my arm and pointed us at the nearest gate. We weren't far. I asked if they knew the name of the road we would come out on to. Not sure. But as we finally came through, at a part of the back end of Highgate I was unfamiliar with, the lad came running back to let us know the name of the street, and also the nearest main drag. He wondered if I wanted him to get us some coffee maybe? He was genuinely concerned for the poor man in the care of a madwoman. So kind, but Hazel was coming. Actually, I'd put her in such a tizz she got a bit lost too. It's now a quarter to six. We'd been walking for two hours. Oh dear me. We sat down on a wall for another little rest and watched a couple of foxes starting on their night patrol. To keep warm we walked further on until we reached the main road and lo and behold, Hazel appeared. As she dropped us back at where I'd parked the car, she looked at me as if fearful for my sanity. 'It's too much ...'

•

THE FOLLOWING EVENING the build-up of tension reached a head. Edwyn's anxiety had reached new heights. He was convinced something very bad was about to happen to him and, to allay his fears, we went off to the casualty department at the Royal Free. All credit to them, they didn't treat us like a pair of hysterics. After all Edwyn had been through there was nothing more natural than to have an episode like this. Their solicitude, coupled with a once-over of his temperature, blood pressure, reactions, etc, completely put his mind at ease. His panic attacks ceased that night and never returned. Natural resilience and an aversion to overreaction held sway. He just needed a little professional reassurance.

Edwyn's late onset seizure, as it was called, turned out to be a not unexpected event. The neurologists prescribed him an anti-convulsant drug, which he remained on for eighteen months. Although they counselled that further seizures were possible, likely even, he had the great good fortune to never have another. We know several people who have had a much more turgid time and may have to put up with the drugs, which can have rotten side effects, for life.

•

2006 WAS LARGELY spent in heads-down, no-nonsense, therapeutic slog. Not very riveting to read about, but quite satisfying to live through, watching Edwyn make steady and determined progress.

Home life hummed steadily along. Will was growing up, sixteen already. He left school that summer and, after a few months' loafing, embarked on a period of work experience at various record companies and film production houses. It helps to have a mother who doesn't mind begging. An awkward age for him and his friends, raring to be out and about, but not old enough to get into places, unless you have a fake ID. So, hordes of teenagers began descending upon us at the weekends. I started calling the middle floor, 'the bachelor wing'. Some mornings I would awake to as many as twelve or fourteen of them lying around the house, under all the spare duvets. I love the smell of testosterone in the morning … That's the first thing, open the windows. Mostly boys, but a few girls, who would be confined to the girls' dormitory, the spare room. One of my rules, no teenage love action. I'm not *that* much a woolly liberal. Edwyn would survey all the teenage activity with an indulgent eye. We both agreed. At least this way, we knew where they were.

I was reminiscing about those times with a few of them recently. They are all grown up now, eighteen, nineteen, with part-time jobs, a few quid, and our place as a doss house is no longer required as their horizons have broadened. The most I ever see overnight these days are four. And that's rare. But I must say, if Will and his mates are anything to go by, the future looks rosy. I'm a big fan of the youth of today.

•

OVER THE MONTHS of 2006 and 2007 Edwyn added a few new activities to his repertoire. He took up Pilates, one-on-one with a guy called Tony, who was great. Lots of stretching and strengthening on equipment slightly resembling torture devices. There's a thing called a reformer which looks a bit like the rack.

Edwyn also had acupuncture, which he wasn't too keen on, although he was very fond of Gary, the acupuncturist, so stuck with it for a while. Historically, Edwyn took a very cynical view of any alternative therapies. At one time my friends, Vanessa and Henri, were both seeing a man who practised something called iridology. This involved looking at your irises and deciding that your spleen was too hot, or something like that. That'll be eighty quid, please. So Edwyn decided to set up a lucrative practice in trendy Queens Park, offering a new therapy of his own devising. Talonology. The idea being you would collect your old toenail clippings, bring them round to his consulting rooms where he would analyse them and diagnose what ailed you. As he went around introducing himself as a talonologist, I can't tell you the number of people who went along with it, fascinated, all the way up to the punch line. He had identified a gap in the market. Vanessa and Henri took his gentle ribbing in very good part.

We were contacted on his MySpace page by a guy called Stewart who specialised in a particular type of yoga. In spite of Edwyn's cynicism, I got in touch with him. Stew and Edwyn have been working together, in our living room, ever since. There's no denying the important contribution

279

the yoga has made to his bendiness (highly technical term, that). He used to be a fixed block, from head to feet. If he turned, everything turned together, as one, including his head. Bending, reaching, stretching, separating the component parts of his body one from the other, these were such hard things for Edwyn to do. He really couldn't attempt these moves without overbalancing. I give a lot of credit to yoga when I see the everyday, *functional* return of his flexibility. The other day he spilt something on the living room floor. As if watching a play, I studied him as he headed for the kitchen for a cloth, came back, reached over right down to the floor to wipe up the puddle, straightened up, *stepped backwards* (incredible to do this without thinking about it), a few paces and wiped again. The hard work, paying off, before my very eyes. Don't underestimate it. When the ability to do trivial little things like this is lost to you, they don't seem trivial any more. And when you get it back, oh, the satisfaction.

A few months back Stewart called me through to witness something he'd been working on for months which had finally happened. Edwyn lowered himself to the floor, unsupported, feet still flat on the ground, left hand behind to catch himself. He then firmly planted his feet and pushed himself off again with the heel of his hand. Slowly, slowly, using his tummy muscles like mad for stability, he raised himself up to a standing position. Try it, it's quite hard for anyone to do. I had no idea he'd come this far. He practises this every day now, with ever-increasing panache. I'm not sure if I'll ever get over the sound of Edwyn the Cynic chanting *Om* and *Shanti* though. The first time I heard it, wafting through to the kitchen where I was holed up, I was actually crying with laughter, fist stuffed in my mouth.

Another member of his team is Edwyn's trainer, Craig. Somehow, something always seems to send us just the right man or woman for the job. Edwyn and Craig are a marriage made in heaven. A rehab specialist, Craig is a man on a mission as far as Edwyn is concerned. He puts him over assault courses, devises exercises that promote new levels of control over his weaker right side, building strength, agility, gently coaxing him to new achievements.

Completing the picture is Sally Ghibaldan, who took over from Trudi in 2007, when Trudi's baby was born. Sally too has been gifted to us. She is simply brilliant. Edwyn, always able to tune in to the good guys, knew he had found what we thought would be impossible – someone to fill Trudi's shoes – from the first hour he spent with her. Therapies of the type that Edwyn has are all about trust and a special rapport. Edwyn is cocooned in the care of the team who have brought him to where he is today. Words are not enough to say thank you.

•

TOWARDS THE END of 2006, it was time to try the studio again. This time, Edwyn's capabilities were very different. He could engage with the process much more, and could offer opinions on the mixes. Seb and he set to work. Seb reckons that as a lot of their old working practices involved wordless communication, born of long familiarity,

281

it wouldn't be too difficult to fall into the way of things once more. He was right. Although there is no denying that Seb is taking more of a leading role than in the old days, he was emphatic that Edwyn was contributing his full share to the partnership. In the space of a month or so, the album was complete. Our old friends, Martin Kelly and Jeff Barrett, co-owners of a long-established record label called Heavenly Recordings, loved the record and took it under their careful wing, where we knew it would get the best care and attention. But equally, Martin and Jeff understood the unique circumstances we would find ourselves in when it came to the promotion of the record.

•

UP UNTIL THIS time, it had been an easy decision to turn down or ignore all requests for interviews about Edwyn's illness, either with Edwyn or me. In the beginning our experience was too intense and far too private to share with newspaper reporters, especially with the type who had probably never heard of him before he got ill. I was not going to subscribe to the, 'Come and wallow with us in our big puddle of misery' school of unsavoury journalism, so beloved of the British press. Inside the music business, our business, I was aware that the word on the street was that Edwyn was in a pretty bad state. Rumours would sometimes find their way back to us. Edwyn was entirely untroubled by this, amused even, as he continued to absorb himself in this complex inner battle for recovery.

I was certainly somewhat more prickly than he about the way the world reacted to him. Back in hospital as I pushed him around in his wheelchair, he attracted stares of morbid curiosity, unpleasant looks often, which I would meet with hostile glares. Other people would studiously avoid looking at us at all. My defensive instinct would kick in and my hackles would rise.

But by late spring 2007, Edwyn had the best answer possible to the misconception that he had been struck down, wiped out, reduced to a shadowy, brain-damaged figure. He had completed his beautiful album, entitled, of course, *Home Again*, and dedicated to Trudi and Ellen. It was, by common consent, one of the finest of his career and he was beside himself with excitement.

The lyrics, as all who have listened to it would agree, are spookily prescient. Many who were not fully aware of Edwyn's problems following his stroke assumed that the whole thing had been written in an emotional response to his illness. But the words and music were complete before the cataclysm of February 2005. Ever the eloquent aphasic, in a recent interview Edwyn has described: '... a sense of foreboding, a sense of agitation', as he worked on it. If so, these were private feelings, not for sharing. Hindsight is pointless, a torment. I can remember vague clues, hints at an inner trouble. But it is too easy, looking back, to magnify the significance of these random remarks; too facile to imbue them with heavy meaning I didn't read at the time. In the last four years I've picked over scraps of conversations, analysed all that went before and regularly beaten myself up in the process. But it's a futile, draining exercise and I'm done with it. We live in the here and now.

Edwyn again: 'Slowly, back towards reality. I've seen the vision, I've seen the light, I've seen experiences worth fighting for. Yes? But bit by bit, I am back in the world. I'm getting better. And more or less I'm getting on with it for the rest of my life.'

•

HEAVENLY RECORDINGS ARE distributed and marketed by EMI and I was invited to go with Jeff and Martin to a strategy meeting at their main office. It was a long time since I had done anything like this and the last time would have been a very different kettle of fish. Twenty or so people sat around a board room table, strangers to me, very professional and extremely courteous all of them, but of course completely in the dark as to what they were to be presented with. I don't get nervous in situations like this at my advanced stage in life. I rather enjoyed it, feeling I was back in our old nutty world, although I almost got an attack of the giggles. The contrast between the world Edwyn and I had been closeted in for two years, a place of mortality and stark realities, and the abiding daftness of the music business – surely by its very nature the definition of *escapism* – was not lost on me.

I enthusiastically reassured them that, although the task of promoting a record with Edwyn's speech and physical difficulties would certainly involve a degree of winging it, especially for Edwyn, he was ready to launch himself at everything he could do to support his record, of which he was terribly proud.

And so we set to work.

Steve Phillips, our new press officer, arranged all interviews with consummate skill. Edwyn's first interviews were with great writers for great magazines and newspapers – people who knew their stuff, did their research, appreciated the record, approached Edwyn and his story with knowledge, with warmth, with respect. No wallowing, no patronising.

Simon Goddard, who had interviewed Edwyn for the release of *The Glasgow School*, which was the last interview he gave before he was robbed of language, spoke to him again now for the *Guardian*, and composed a biographical piece, bringing his story up to date. Danny Ecclestone wrote an exhaustive piece for *Mojo* magazine, talking to Edwyn and me over two sessions and placing Edwyn's present in the context of his past.

Craig McLean, a great writer whom we have known for a long time, wrote his article for a couple of publications, including the *Glasgow Herald*. (Some time in the 90s I received my raucous introduction to proper gin martinis at the Sunset Marquis hotel in LA in the company of this good-time guy. I'm not sure how Edwyn and I made it to the airport the next day. I only remember the terrible pain.)

We started off doing the interviews with me in attendance, to interpret, I suppose. Edwyn's speech style was halting, difficult. I could prompt, draw him out, anticipate what he was trying to say if he was struggling, follow where

285

he lead. And provide some background information, shading in the detail that Edwyn would struggle with. But before too long Edwyn tried to manage on his own. The second half of the interview with Danny, for instance, was conducted alone. I'm so grateful to these guys for the way they spoke to Edwyn and especially for the way they wrote their pieces. The conversations he had with them and the way they represented him in print made him feel restored to his former self and gave him a giant boost.

Edwyn progressed to broadcast interviews, organised by the redoubtable Tina Skinner, an EMI promotions manager of vast experience. He was interviewed across all the major radio stations, and on television, some recorded, some going out live, and managed it all with total aplomb.

Two interviews he did, where I thought he was on blistering form, stand out in my memory: one for Channel 4 News with Stephanie West, beautifully filmed in his studio, which showed Edwyn off in his best possible light, and one with Robert Elms, a contemporary of Edwyn's, for BBC Radio London. Edwyn had been interviewed by him many times in the past, so there was comfort and familiarity there. Edwyn found a fluency with Robert, expressing his ideas with great clarity and simplicity.

All of these encounters were a first for Edwyn and a first for most of the people interviewing him: a man with aphasia, with the effects of a stroke still clearly visible on him, but alive and vital, declaring to the world that there was life beyond brain injury, giving a good account of himself, striding forth once more. Well, that's what I saw. He was more

impressive to me now than when he was young and hand-
some, fully able, in his prime and sweeping all before him.

•

So I stood on the edge of my world
At a place where the sky meets the sea
But my haven was a cauldron of bile
For the sea was bewitched and defiled
There's a passage leads down to the sea
There's a step for each day of the year
They are ancient, but they've stood the test of time
Those who venture need have little to fear
~ Leviathan, 2004

IN SUMMER 2004, six months prior to his illness, Edwyn
had made a film for Scottish Television called *Home for the
Holidays*, about Helmsdale and its environs, extolling its
wonders and endeavouring to explain its hold on him. (Our
friend Elizabeth Fraser tells of a phone call she received
from an elderly woman in Lybster, Caithness: 'Who's his
grandfather? (Edwyn had referred several times in the
prgramme to Dr Mackintosh without mentioning him by
name) Edwyn's done more in this programme for the area
than the tourist board ever did!')

The film was made by a producer and director, Fiona
Buchanan and Paul Tucker, who had faithfully kept in
touch with Edwyn's fight back to strength. In 2006, they
began to journey regularly to London to film him and his
progress. Edwyn was very keen on this idea, mainly as it

would give him a tangible record of his achievements as he moved forward. I always meant to keep a video record of sorts but this is one my many hopeless areas. I take very few photographs, use the video camera even more rarely, accidentally delete the few things I do record, struggle ineptly with the ever-changing demands of technology and mostly just give up. The idea that I am now the family and career archivist fills me with dread. The other difficulty is that as soon as I point a camera at Edwyn he invariable waves a dismissive hand at me and says, 'Switch it off …'

So, Fiona and Paul to the rescue. I believe they would have done the filming just for our private consumption but Edwyn was very happy that it should be offered up for broadcast, and the BBC ended up commissioning the film, with the full understanding that it would be made over a lengthy period of time, which turned out to be fifteen months. It's fascinating to look at it now, as I can see that Edwyn has come on leaps and bounds since its start. It follows him through family life both in London and Helmsdale, as Edwyn worked with his therapists, and as he tackled a couple of gargantuan challenges.

•

THE FIRST OF these challenges was something else I used to bring up with Edwyn while he was in hospital.

'Wait and see, one day we'll get down the steps again, Edwyn.'

I have to admit, this was said more in hope than expectation back then. The steps in question were the Whalligoe

Steps, a name of Norse extraction given to a dramatic cove with high cliff sides in Caithness. The steps are man-made and go back a few hundred years to when the place was a natural harbour for small herring fishing boats, and the local population had to devise a way of accessing the inaccessible. They cut a zigzagging course of stone steps down the cliff. God knows how. I look at them in disbelief at the perseverance and audacity of men. Still in use until the 1950s, the steps are only visited nowadays by those who actively seek them out. They are not on the official tourist information, presumably for safety reasons. Edwyn immortalised the place in a song called 'Leviathan', on his new album. (Trudi enquired about the name of this song one day. After a studied think, Edwyn replied, 'A mythical sea monster.' Again, one of those shocking moments when the aphasia was held at bay and Edwyn expressed himself descriptively and succinctly.)

After a pilgrimage to the steps on New Year's Day 2004, a day when they looked at their glowering and imposing best, Edwyn came up with a brooding melody and the words above which capture the atmosphere of the place perfectly. I'm not sure he would have included among those who 'need have little to fear' people dealing with the after-effects of stroke. But we had developed such a good two-man stair technique that, during a trip in April 2007 when the film crew joined us, I was confident we could have a crack at it. With the crew in attendance, we would have enough people on hand in case of difficulty.

It was a bitter day, featuring Edwyn's weather nemesis, the wind. But down we got, halfway anyway, and the dramatic sight of the place, the cliffs, the sea, the birds, was a tremendous affirmation of how far he'd come. He made the climb back up without even stopping to rest, to the cheers of the crew and Davie, the local resident and chief custodian of the steps. Davie will happily give any visitor the full history of the place; a real labour of love. We returned on a much more benign, sunny day in August, with my brother David in tow, and this time we made it all the way to the bottom. Davie met us again at the top. Each time we return Edwyn gets the VIP welcome from this great character.

•

FOR THE SECOND landmark event, Paul and Fiona scurried down from Glasgow to record Edwyn's return to the rehearsal room with his band.

On the journey back south in January 2007, after our northerly sojourn for the Christmas holidays to Helmsdale, two years on from his stroke, Edwyn began to sing. The song he sang was a very old one of his own, called 'Poor Old Soul'. It was written about Alan Horne, the founder of Postcard Records.

He sang the entire first verse.

Back with a vengeance, much in vogue
To wit: the harlequin, the rogue
Befriending the meek

His tongue tucked firmly in his cheek
You better come clean
How can anybody be so mean?
You better come clean
I will not be a party to your scheme

I wasn't aware that he had recovered the ability to remember lyrics until that moment.

'Have you been practising on the sly?'

'I have, you know.' Fairly smug.

So I decided to challenge him with another of his songs 'Make Me Feel Again'. I had to lead him into each line and he needed lots of prompting. But rather like it was when he began drawing, the potential seemed clear. He was going to sing again. All we had to do was build up his repertoire, one song at a time.

Our method for this was quite straightforward. I typed out the lyrics, big print, lots of spacing. Edwyn would murmur them aloud while listening to the track. Then, when he had established the arrangement again in his head, he'd move on to simply singing the song over and over again until the words began to stick. This took a lot of practise. A lot. He would sit at the kitchen table and work. The main problem was missing the start of each line. There was no way to overcome this but endless repetition. And when he moved on to another song, he would have to remember to keep his hand in with the ones he had already practised, lest all the hard work should simply evaporate. This holds true to this very day. Since January 2007 there has not been a day that goes by that Edwyn does not practise his songs. These days he sings his entire set, twice over, every day. He races through it at top speed, checking it's all in order. He is emphatic, and I wouldn't dispute it, that if he doesn't keep this mental top-up going, the whole lot will simply fly away and he'll be back to square one.

I should mention that Edwyn's return to singing coincided with Will deciding to pick up a guitar for the first time. The sound of a teenager learning an instrument is something that has to be endured in the early stages. So he would be plink plonking away, making millions of dissonant mistakes, in one corner of the house, and Edwyn would be doing something similar, stop-start singing, in another corner. And this would go on every single night. If I am to be completely honest, I did have to keep reminding myself of how wonderful it was to have the chance to live around this cacophony, and resist the urge to run screaming out of the house away from the racket. How soon we forget! I would wander around, muttering through clenched teeth: 'Cause for celebration, cause for celebration ...'

By April, he had learned six songs sufficiently well for us to convene the band and see him have a go at being the front man once more. In the band, friends and stalwarts, Andy Hackett, Paul Cook, Carwyn Ellis and Sean Read, with James Walbourne taking on Edwyn's guitar playing duties.

It is so interesting for me to look at the footage of that first rehearsal and see Edwyn; tentative, halting, stumbling. But at the time we, all of us, band, film crew, Will and I, were jubilant. It was an encouraging beginning and it left

Edwyn with a clear idea of the task ahead. It wasn't complicated, just non-stop practise.

●

AFTER A COUPLE more practise sessions with the band,
Edwyn retired to the kitchen table to grind it out on his
own. He set himself a goal. To be sufficiently improved to
appear at a few small shows in London in November. To
face public scrutiny and see if performing could become
part of his vista of the future.

The intervening months were spent in continuing to
work to promote his album, including making a video for
his first single in many years. The way he handled it, you
would have thought he'd never been away. We enjoyed a
few weeks break in Helmsdale before rejoining the band
for rehearsals in the autumn. James had other commitments
by this time so we needed to find a guitar player to take his
place. When Andy suggested that we ask Roddy Frame, we
couldn't possibly have imagined anyone better. Roddy and
Edwyn have been friends since they were label mates on
Postcard Records, way back at the beginning of their
careers. Roddy had been sixteen, a guitar-playing and song-
writing prodigy when Postcard was lucky enough to find
him and his band, Aztec Camera. He was seventeen when
I first met him, excited to be in London and the proud new
owner of a beautiful Gibson semi-acoustic guitar. Edwyn
and Roddy had lived out their careers in parallel. Although
sometimes they wouldn't see each other for a while, their
friendship had endured. The two of them shared a great

deal of past history, reference points, highs and lows. I wasn't sure Roddy would feel able to do this though and didn't want him pressurised. But I was totally wrong. He was in like Flynn, completely committed.

Paul, too, had had to heed the call of other commitments. He was a Sex Pistol once more, the band having reformed for a big tour. His place was taken by Dave Ruffy, another old amigo with whom Edwyn had played in the early years of his solo career. Dave's long and illustrious drumming career had also included drumming with Aztec Camera for a number of years, and when Edwyn recorded his first solo album, *Hope and Despair*, in Cologne, Dave and Roddy had both been there to help him. So they were an incestuous lot. But every member of his band were straight out of the top drawer and their dedication to providing Edwyn with a perfect backing was total. The idea was that Edwyn's shows would be as good musically as ever. No quarter would be asked for or need be given.

Edwyn worked very hard at getting an increasingly better flow to his vocals. He was now up to fourteen songs, a full set. But there is more to a show than just getting the words in the right order. Nobody knew better than Edwyn that a performance is composed of certain intangibles. You almost have to forget yourself in the process. But how could he do that when he had to concentrate so hard on keeping the words together? Again, it would come down to sheer hard graft. Practise, practise, practise.

We had booked a small theatre in the West End, the Arts Theatre, for two shows at the end of November 2007.

But before that, Edwyn was asked to take part in the BBC Electric Proms, an annual multi-venue event that the BBC records for broadcast. Edwyn's show was to be at Dingwalls, a club with a lot of history in Camden that holds about six hundred people, on Sunday 30 October. So the deadline moved forward.

I have to come clean now. These months were not all euphoria and achievement. As the time for Edwyn baring his all in public approached, I was struggling. There was a great deal going on, a lot of responsibility and I was feeling the pressure. A part of me was wondering if I was doing the right thing, allowing Edwyn to be so exposed to scrutiny. I know this was not my decision, it was Edwyn's, but I had a great deal of power in this new life of ours and I was horribly worried that I might be abusing it, by going along with him into something that might turn out to be a bridge too far. My job was to protect my family, not expose them to potential dangers. As the first show got closer and closer, I felt sick with anxiety.

•

WHEN EDWYN WAS marooned in hospital I would sometimes allow myself to daydream about a day when he might play again. And then I would pull myself up short, because it seemed like such an impossibility and it was cruel to torment myself with such thoughts. But in my daydream it was an unalloyed joy to see Edwyn perform again. And here it was happening in real life and all I could feel was a bald terror. What was wrong? If I really thought, I knew that I was only a little afraid it would all go horribly wrong. But I had such faith in Edwyn I didn't really see that happening. Doing a little amateur psychology, I think I was afraid to let go. I'd been holding on so tight, and now I had to let go and he would do this thing entirely alone. But whatever the cause of my anxiety, it was spoiling the build-up to the big night for me. I kept all these thoughts from Edwyn, of course. His confidence in himself, his belief that he could pull it off, was everything.

·

ALL THREE SHOWS sold out in about two minutes flat (an exaggeration, but near enough), the last rehearsal took place and the day of the Elecric Proms dawned bright and clear. Well, absolutely pissing down with rain, actually, but you can't have everything. When we assembled at the gig for the sound check, our old friends, Fiona and Paul, were there with their film crew. As they recorded the activity – and I've seen the footage – I can see how tense I looked. But no matter, everyone else, including Edwyn, appeared to be full of excitement and anticipation. Actually, the sound check relaxed me a lot, it passed off so well.

I had, of course, an impossibly long guest list, but the organisers were in the mood to indulge me. It seemed like almost everybody we cared about was there. Nan and David had come from Scotland. Edwyn's family were to join us for the next show in November.

Many people have described the tense atmosphere among the audience as they waited for Edwyn's appearance.

So it wasn't just me – everyone was somewhat apprehensive about how they would find him. His old self on-stage was an unpredictable wit, a raconteur. Many people came as much for his stage patter as they did for the music. There was a palpable tension as they waited for him to appear.

As I should have known, they found him just where he wanted to be. In his element. The old ham that he is, he saved his best for the show. His fear was turned towards the focus of performance. He had never sung this well in rehearsal. He laughed, he managed several exchanges with the audience, and wallowed in their reaction. The band was wonderful, surrounding him with expert accompaniment but also loads of moral support. The set flew by, building to a wonderful frenetic ending, and received with a terribly moving ovation.

I was whirling, could barely take it in. Afterwards, it was something of a blur of friends, relief, euphoria and a great deal of champagne. Only Edwyn and our teetotal son escaped the hangover of the next day. I felt drunk before I'd touched a drop. (David and Hazel were cross with themselves the next day, but felt much better when they realised that there was hardly a soul who had escaped unscathed; all were caught up in the exhilaration of the moment.)

For David and Hazel, who had been there on so many of the bad days, to see Edwyn pull off a performance the way he did was a heady sensation. As they watched him, other scenes had flashed through their minds, and the comparison was almost incredible. David who had sat beside me as the stroke consultant told us we had to accept that Edwyn's chances of significant recovery were poor. David helping him pick a runner in the Grand National as we tried to keep our spirits up when he was crushed by infection on the brink of rehab. And then there was Hazel by Edwyn's hospital bedside during those first days, when he was still pretty out of it, reassuring him that his eBay feedback (100% positive) was still intact. She knew his password and had checked for outstanding transactions. We couldn't tell if he had a clue what we were talking about, but the real Edwyn would have fretted to think that his seven-year perfect record was falling apart. He had two things that needed paying for. One was a used Elvin Bishop T-shirt (which said BIG FUN on it) and the other was a vintage Levi country and western shirt; red checks with cactus plants. The T-shirt remains his favourite to this day. And the country shirt was on his back at Dingwalls that very evening.

All the therapy team were there in force: Virginia, his physio, who had taken over from Ellen when she returned to Australia; yoga-ace Stewart; Tony Pilates; Gary the acupuncturist; Craig, the fantastic new physical trainer; Trudi with her husband Alex, stealing a rare night out since baby Scarlett was born and Sally, her brilliant successor. How strange for them to see him in this setting, sucking up the praise, master of all he surveyed. They all had a hand in getting him here and we celebrated together in style, together with the band and a cast of what seemed like hundreds of friends. I woke up the next morning, turned round and looked at Edwyn through my fog, and wondered if I had dreamt it. Mind boggling. His Highness remained serene: 'I did it, at last. I'm well again.'

•

WE MOVED TO the next two shows; Edwyn was brimful of confidence and I was a little more relaxed. With each show he has done his appetite for performing has grown, his self-assurance has soared and his ability to deliver improved beyond question.

Edwyn loves a good review. There are many people who claim they never read their reviews. Prior to his stroke (and I'll wager not much has changed), Edwyn had a forensic memory for every review he had practically ever had, particularly the bad ones. He was a bit of a one for holding a grudge.

If you asked him how he felt about constructive criticism he would insist there was no such thing. Backstage after a show you sometimes get a certain type of fan that thinks that if they shoot from the hip, lob a few put-downs your way, then the object of their fascination will somehow admire them for their forthrightness. In their deluded state they imagine he will turn to them and say, 'Thank you for your refreshing candour. Endless praise is so tedious. You, on the other hand, are interesting. Let's be friends for ever.'

The reality is more likely to be: 'I see, you're one of those, are you?'

I've got less patience than Edwyn for this sort of thing. I waste no time in steering these 'fans' politely out the door.

'Give me blanket sycophancy every time.' I'm quoting him directly.

In the aftermath of each show since his return, Edwyn could bask in lots of lovely positive affirmation. And each reviewer was at pains to stress that they were not making allowances:

Pete Paphides, *The Times*, November 2007:
It might be a cliché, but it's also true: you really don't know how fond you are of someone until they're gone. Or, in the case of Edwyn Collins – back in action two years after a near-fatal stroke – nearly gone. By way of proof, the 300 people who filled this small West End theatre raised the roof as Collins, aided by a walking stick, gingerly made his way to the stool where he sat for the next hour. Loud cheers for what the sometime front man had been through were only natural. But with yet a note to be played, you wondered if, by the end, it would be just his bravery they were applauding.

As misgivings go, this one couldn't have been more fleeting. It's tempting to say that the Caledonian funk of 'Poor Old Soul' was exactly as it sounded in 1981when it first appeared on the fledgling Postcard imprint. In fact, Collins's band – which included his old Aztec Camera chum, Roddy Frame and the former Ruts drummer, David Ruffy – invested the music with a *joie de vivre* that seemed to flush the place free of sentimentality. For his lean, adrenalised fretwork on 'Falling and Laughing' and his protracted tremolo abuse on 'What Presence?!', Frame was a revelation, doing the work that his friend had once been able to take care of himself.

With just the singing to concentrate on, Collins stumbled slightly on the middle-eight of Orange Juice's 1983 hit 'Rip It Up', but then the concentration of words constituted a mouthful when he was in his twenties.

The songs from *Home Again* – the album that Collins recorded but didn't get around to releasing before his stroke – tapped into a more contemplative vein. In particular, the title track elicited a holy shiver, partly because of the beatific baritone conferred upon it by the singer and partly because the words unfurled from the stage like a present from the younger Collins to his future self.

It seems Collins is even writing again. Not the wordy, worldly, ruminations of yore but, in the case of 'Searching For the Truth', haiku-like hymns of gratitude to consciousness itself. In a pop year already heaving with re-formations and resurrections, this was something else entirely.

Short of an intimate acoustic show by Lord Lucan, it was the comeback against which all comebacks must surely be measured.

Paul Morley, The *Observer*, April 2008:
It's not possible to talk about Edwyn Collins's

confident, charismatic and pretty audacious 90-minute performance at the Shepherds Bush Empire without mentioning that, in many ways, he is slowly learning to be himself again. It would be great just to celebrate the tart, zesty songs, more than one of which are absolute pop classics; his crack backing band featuring a gloriously frisky Aztec Camera's Roddy Frame on guitar; and his mischievous sense of humour.

The reality is, though, that after suffering two catastrophic strokes in 2005, Collins almost died, and he is performing live again as part of his battle to rebuild his life, his mind, his memory and personality, and to continue the fight back to physical and mental strength ... Only when he sings, deep and sure, fearlessly piecing together his shattered past, does he seem totally in control of himself, and the disorientating world around him.

Collins perches on top of a speaker, looking sleek in show-business suit and tie, relishing the fact that the music he's had to learn all over again is actually pretty damn good. He clearly enjoys his role as brainy, darkly romantic crooner, even as he's still feeling his way towards fully understanding it. He loves hearing the skinny, pale Frame play unlikely, post-Prince guitar hero on his behalf. The thoughtful, intoxicating, awkwardly graceful songs Collins wrote as a member of early-1980s pop pioneers Orange Juice as an adventurous solo singer, culminating in his magnificent mid-1990s hit 'A Girl Like You', are delivered with an inevitable, uncanny freshness.

It is an insight into his extraordinary determination, and lack of bitterness and self-pity, that the show isn't a painful, disconcerting exercise in sentimentality, or something even odder and sadder, but a buoyant and inspiring performance that never once suffers from a failure of nerve or a loss of concentration. You can't avoid the reality of Collins's condition, but it doesn't get in the way of what he really wants us to think about. His songs.

There were many more in the same vein. It was gratifying to see the depth of understanding of Edwyn's endeavours. That the writers read him so accurately, and delivered such elegant appraisals of his shows, was perfectly satisfying for Edwyn. Grist to his mill, indeed.

Of course, Edwyn's appearance as he arrives on stage now is somewhat different to his pre-stroke self. And his speech is different. As he regularly puts it: 'My speech is dodgy, but my singing is wonderful.'

This has led only two reviewers to question whether someone like Edwyn should be allowed out in public. I'm paraphrasing them a trifle harshly, but that was what they meant, more or less. I, and everyone else who has seen what he does, say phooey to that. What Edwyn does by confronting the world and forcing his way back to his old life is to demystify, to remove the stigma of stroke and brain injury, which is a big deal. When you meet him for the first time, you notice the stroke effects. It takes a little time to get a handle on how they work on him. When you meet him for the second time, you can forget about them. Pragmatic, unflinching, energetic, upbeat, he puts you at your ease. He made the decision to get back to work. It gives his life shape and meaning. Edwyn blanks out the negative, because it's not useful to him. He has always been implacable in the face of criticism. He has never practised self-recrimination. He lives a blame-free life.

Before I paint too saintly a picture of him, he's able to do this partly because of the personality traits I have found less appealing historically: self-absorption, tunnel vision, stubbornness, cussedness. And they are all back with a vengeance, having taken a sabbatical while he was in the depths of his illness. And this is again cause for celebration, I have to keep telling myself. He's back in all his glory, taking me for granted, oblivious to the mountains of detail I plough through.

•

I AM FAMOUSLY inefficient, disorganised, and a champion procrastinator. Yet I am the designated head of all the boring stuff of life in this family. And, for twenty-five years, I have been making a pig's ear of it. I forget birthdays, flight times, VAT returns, details big and small, business and domestic. Everything is done in a panic at the last minute. I hate it. I need a manager. But I am the manager. The world's worst manager, he used to call me. But, in the absence of a more suitable candidate, it falls to me by default to be service robot. I have an optimistic disposition. I get there in the end.

I refer to Edwyn as the man who has not paid a phone bill since 1980. He does not trouble his mind with minutiae of that sort. Yet, he could organise major technical projects like his recording studio, down to the most minor detail. Selective, you see. William, son of Edwyn, aged nineteen as I write this, is shaping up to follow nicely in his father's footsteps. He is neither use nor ornament (as my mother would say), but can be transformed into a dynamo when engaged in a project that absorbs him. Which includes nothing in the way of domesticity. Left home alone recently, he was telling me on the phone about his plans for dinner: 'So, I'm going to shove it in that thing, you know, with the door, under the cooker.'

'You mean the oven?'

'Yeah, yeah, that.'

He's nineteen. It's frightening. What on earth is to become of him?

But then again, his father made his way without acquiring too many of these skills. He once had a huge argument with me about whether or not it's possible to wring a cloth out with one hand. Now he only has the use of one hand, I have to concede defeat. My own father had a very apt, smug expression he often used: 'It's not often I'm wrong, but I'm right again …'

That's Edwyn. Towering self-belief.

•

THROUGHOUT 2008, WE took to the road again (Edwyn's appetite for work in every form is insatiable. I'm dragged along in his wake, often grumpy and complaining, longing for retirement, but mostly very grateful that the work ethic so apparent in his grandfather has surfaced in Edwyn when he needs it most. I cannot complain about working too hard when he is leading the charge and the work has saved his life).

We toured the UK in April and went to Paris. In Glasgow and Edinburgh, Edwyn was cheered to the rafters by his homecoming audience. In his old favourite stomping grounds of Manchester and Leeds and Birmingham, he was welcomed back by old friends, show promoters and audiences alike. He walked out onto the stage at Shepherd's Bush Empire looking like he'd never been away, wearing his natty charity shop Dior suit and his yellow ochre shoes, carrying his silver-topped cane that I bought him for Christmas, and delivered his most flawless singing performance yet. We had parties after lots of the shows and he never flagged. Across the summer we played at a handful of festivals in the UK and Europe.

Edwyn was famously sceptical about summer festivals, arising from his punk rock roots. One of his crowd-pleasers is a song called 'The Campaign for Real Rock', which is a seven-minute tirade against hippy festivals both old and new, culminating in a refrain which starts as a whisper and swells to a roar:

Yes, yes, yes it's the summer festival
The truly detestable summer festival...

When he found himself, unaccountably, on-stage at Glastonbury, the ultimate hippy heartland, he indulged himself in a chorus or two of the old spiteful anthem. But in a good-humoured way. And, he had to grudgingly admit, he really had a rather wonderful time. The reception from the crowd would have brought a tear to a glass eye. He returned to the Highlands to play with his band at a wonderful festival near Beauly in Invernesshire, called Belladrum. In a packed tent, with a large contingent of the Helmsdale friends of all ages, including the teenagers, down in front of the stage, on a Saturday night in August, I felt everything come together in a way that made sense of all we had been through. I hung back on my own in the middle of the crowd, among strangers, and as I watched Edwyn smiling happily at his band, at the fantastic audience, at Will jumping around like a maniac stage side, I felt the world stand still for a moment and my fear finally dissolve. Who gets happy endings like these? Not many. I don't know that we deserved it, because I have met too many others who deserve far better than life metes out to them. But, deserving or not, I was ready to accept the giddy happiness of this summer night.

•

BRAIN DAMAGE IS a terrifying subject, I know that. The unthinkable thing. It's natural to recoil at the mere thought of it impinging on your world. But Edwyn, Will and I had joined the ranks of those for whom it was real life, not a bogey man. We have been very scared, but that has passed. I didn't care for the idea that we had become

307

objects of sympathy. Not that I dwelt on it, we had too much going on, but sometimes something would happen or something would be said that made me realise that there might be a perception abroad that life had deposited Edwyn by the roadside, that he was a poor, washed-up unfortunate. There is no self-pity in this family, no enviousness of other people's lives.

I remember asking Edwyn many years ago if he had ever wished he were someone else. He never had and neither had I, even at times when things were most definitely not swinging in our direction. Edwyn's illness hasn't changed that conviction. We still love being us.

Every week brings forth new adventures, fresh opportunities. And *still* Edwyn improves. There is no sign of that horrible 'plateau' the doctors talked about, which I dreaded so. I don't believe it will ever happen.

•

ON THE DAYS around the fourth anniversary of his stroke, Edwyn produced yet more evidence of his return to power. One evening recently he turned his computer towards me and asked: 'Is that right?'

In reply to an email from a well-wisher, he had written:

Dear Caroline

Strokes are hard. I'm getting there. 'Home Again' is a good album. Andrew is a good friend too. Smithfield you brought too? Cheerio for now.

Love Edwyn

I stared at this miniature masterpiece and silently took in the achievement. He had addressed each and every point Caroline had brought up. He had found the words he needed in his head. He had translated them into written form, previously an impossibility. Even his punctuation was perfect. Doggedly working away on his own, he had reached these dizzy heights. Two years ago, one year ago, I could not have envisaged this degree of independent writing.

In September last, Edwyn played a show at the Purcell Room at the Southbank Centre in London to celebrate Heavenly Recordings' eighteenth birthday. The next morning, a Sunday, Edwyn was up with the lark. By the time I came down, he'd made a pot of coffee and a fried-egg toasted sandwich for himself. That might not seem like much compared to performing on stage to a packed crowd. But he hadn't used the frying pan in three and a half years. We both had a celebratory jig round the kitchen.

·

BOTH OF THE above stories are examples of how therapy and persistence translate into everyday, functional living. Edwyn's progress is composed of hundreds of these little victories. Long may they continue.

In the days and weeks following his release from hospital Edwyn would turn to me and announce, out of the blue, 'It's my life. I'm Edwyn. This is me. I don't want to die. I want to live for ever.' Now he often reflects: 'A first, I think. What I've done, with my stroke. I must get better. I will get better.'

•

AND HE HAS. And he will. These days, we walk in the sun.

2007